SPEED,

ALWAYS IN YOUR CORNER.

INTENTIONAL FOCUS.

REFRAME ATTACK.

SPARTAN DAWGS.

NOW. WE. GO.

THE STANDARD

WINNING Every Day at YOUR Highest Level

BEN NEWMAN

Advance Praise for The STANDARD...

There are very few people you meet in life who come in swiftly and completely, causing you to level up instantly to inspire better, communicate clearer and teach you to create massive impact. Ben is hands down the master at this. Ben, like this book, is transformative and trustworthy.

Dr. Gabrielle Lyon
Founder of the Institute of Muscle-Centric Medicine®

In "The Standard," Ben Newman lays out a clear and concise roadmap for incorporating standards into your life to achieve more happiness, success, and peace of mind. Ben teaches readers the tactics and strategies peak performers have used for decades to create a mindset that engages thoughts with actions to produce optimal results in all areas of your life. In addition to thoroughly exploring what standards are, Ben gives readers several practical examples of how to put this philosophy to work in the boardroom, on the playing field, in your relationships, and in all other parts of your life.

Ed Mylett
Global Speaker and Peak Performance Expert and Bestselling Author of *The Power of One More*

Ben Newman does it again! He is masterful in his ability to break down big-picture concepts into every day, meaningful changes each of us can make to achieve the greatness that is inside of us. The Standard is a way of life. Ben not only provides examples of the standard in action, but he also maps a course that allows each of us to find and implement the standard philosophy in our own lives. If you are looking to elevate your life, your relationships, and your career, this is the book for you!

Stephanie White

Head Coach Connecticut Sun

Consistency is one of the truest measurements of performance and Ben Newman CONSISTENTLY lives to a higher STANDARD. This book is no exception! We should all aim to become a better version of ourselves each day, if you dare to be great, read "THE STANDARD!"

Ted Rath

Vice President of Player Performance Philadelphia Eagles

"The Standard" is a transformative masterpiece that provides the tools and motivation to unlock your true potential and elevate your life. With practical advice, relatable anecdotes, and actionable steps, it offers a comprehensive roadmap to becoming the best version of yourself. Ben Newman's wisdom and storytelling make it feel like a personal mentor guiding you through self-discovery.

Amberly Lago

Expert Mindset Coach, Bestselling Author and Keynote Speaker

Ben Newman has helped some of the world's top athletes, teams, and businesses improve their standards and achieve incredible results, and in his new book, "The Standard," he unveils how the secrets and strategies to leveling up so readers can experience their own personal and professional success.

Drew Hanlen

Top NBA Skills Coach and Author of *Stop Bullshitting Yourself*

"The Standard" IS the Standard and nobody personifies that more than Ben Newman. This is not just a MINDSET for Ben but a LIFESTYLE, an IDENTITY. If you're looking to level up, Ben is the one to coach you up and The STANDARD is the book for you.

Jim Rome

Radio Hall of Fame and Host of The Jim Rome Show – CBS Sports Radio

To become a world champion, you must live to standards. Finally, the book has been written to help you build your standards. Discipline and standards won me a gold medal. Period. That is how winning is done. Now it is your turn.

Justin Gatlin

Olympic Gold Medalist and Former World's Fastest Man

Ben Newman doesn't just teach elite performers about excellence; he lives it as well. His book will show you how to set the highest standards for yourself, and achieve them.

Tim Grover

World Champion Performance Coach and CEO of ATTACK Athletics, Inc.

The Standard

WINNING Every Day at YOUR Highest Level

Ben Newman

Published by Game Changer Publishing

Paperback ISBN: 978-1-961189-46-1
Hardcover ISBN: 978-1-961189-50-8
Digital: ISBN: 978-1-961189-51-5

www.GameChangerPublishing.com

For our children,

J. Isaac and Kennedy Rose. My mother-your grandmother-

instilled a BURN in me to own it every day

and to live to the STANDARD.

I pray I live the same example for YOU one day at a time.

In loving memory of

Janet Fishman Newman

Bret Colson, my esteemed editor: you are truly incredible. I can't thank you enough for how YOU challenge me and how YOU attack our partnership. Your commitment, passion, eagle eye, writing, and attention to detail have made "The STANDARD" the STANDARD.

When your mind is telling you that you're done,
that you're exhausted, that you cannot possibly
go any farther, you're actually only 40% done.
—David Goggins, *Can't Hurt Me*

Table of Contents

Foreword

by Jon Gordon

Ben Newman and I have known each other for more than 15 years. During this time he has become more than a friend. He has become a brother.

I've watched Ben grow in his influence and impact and one of my favorite principles he teaches is Standard over feelings. When you set a standard in your life the decisions you make are done according to standard not the feelings you have in the moment. The truth is your feelings will often say you should give up or give less than your best but the standard you set always requires your best. As someone who teaches leadership and develops leaders around the world I always encourage leaders to set the standard. When everyone on your team and in your organization knows the standard you can lead to the standard. If someone's performance falls short of the standard you can point to the standard and show them the discrepancy or gap between their work and the standard. It actually makes leading much more effective and simpler.

Because I know how important it is to set the Standard I am thrilled that Ben has written this book. We both believe that people can transform and elevate their lives, work and team when they learn the value of introducing a standards-based philosophy.

We're not alone in this belief. Many people in the peak performance field widely recognize that standards, implemented with faith, discipline, and direction, are essential for meeting and exceeding financial, health, and relationship goals. But because teaching others about the importance of standards is second nature to many of us, until now, nobody has taken the time to fully explore the genesis of what standards are, how they are created, and the power they hold in creating dynamic and positive outcomes.

That is what makes The Standard so timely and essential. Through our work with some of the world's top athletes, teams, and companies, Ben and I have seen the results that standards produce. From boardrooms to locker rooms, with goals of every size and in all facets of life, standards produce results.

In clear and concise steps, The Standard sets the standard about what you should know in implementing this valuable process to drive results in your life and in others. Page after page reveals how to create and execute standards in precise detail, backed by several examples of how standards have produced outsized results for some of the world's highest achievers.

The Standard is the valuable blueprint you need to guide you to breakthroughs in all parts of your life. Set the standard and you'll raise your performance and leadership to a much higher level.

-Jon Gordon
15x Best-selling author of The Energy Bus and Training Camp
JonGordon.com

Introduction

Many tactics, strategies, and philosophies are tied to peak performance. Most reflect the unique experiences and accomplishments that high achievers, experts, and others have used to succeed in their relationships, businesses, on athletic fields, and many other parts of their lives.

However, a handful of these strategies are foundational baselines you must implement if you want the same results. At the top of that list is the need to create standards in your life.

In *The Standard*, I've analyzed what it takes to create effective standards and joined them with essential lessons I've learned and taught in my eighteen years as a performance coach. I wanted to explore this concept deeply to give you the critical knowledge to implement *The Standard* into your life for outsized results.

To help you master this principle, I've identified two dozen essential elements you can use in any situation to create practical, meaningful, and achievable standards. When you build these standards into your life, you won't focus on outcomes. Instead, faithfully and consistently doing what a standard requires of you will create a natural progression that will lead you to the desired results. *The*

Standard teaches you to focus on processes you can fully control instead of win-and-loss outcomes you can't.

I've also given you several examples of standards in action so that you can better understand the universal nature of standards and why they should be an essential part of your success game plan. You're about to get a behind-the-scenes look at why standards are an integral part of the world's most successful companies and sports franchises.

The Standard is blunt and direct, requiring you to look at your life differently than before. If you're not getting the outcomes you want, owning your life starts with owning the processes down to the smallest details. You must be intensely focused, committed, and ready to push yourself hard, without reservation, to create process-based standards to win.

I only had one standard in writing this book. I wanted to teach you what it takes to win every damn day by giving you the knowledge, desire, and drive you need to see your standards transform your life forever.

If you're ready, *The Standard* will do just that.

NOW. WE. GO.

CHAPTER 1

Mastering The STANDARD

In the summer of 2014, I began working with running back Jonas Gray at the New England Patriots' pre-season training camp.

While there, I witnessed the most incredible display of what it means to live your life with The Standard in place. That is where I saw, up close and personal, the brilliant mind, leadership, and dedicated work ethic of Tom Brady.

Countless stories have been written about Brady over the years. He defines the word "champion" in every sense. What I saw during that season confirmed all those stories you've heard about him…and more.

By this time in his career, Tom's reputation was already cast in stone as the GOAT. Based on what he had already achieved in his career, many people might assume that he would ease up a bit and enjoy the few remaining years of his star-studded career. Few people could have imagined at that point that he would play at his top level for almost another decade.

I suspect he couldn't have guessed he would play twenty-three seasons in the NFL. Another part of me believes Tom would not be surprised by how long he brought everything he had on the way to playing in ten Super Bowls, winning seven of them.

In that summer of 2014, I traveled to the Washington Redskins training facility, where they were holding a joint three-day camp with the Patriots. In addition to working with Jonas Gray, I was there working with Will Compton and some of the other Redskins, so my work afforded me the opportunity of watching the Pats practice as well.

As the Pats walked out of their locker room, I noticed you could cut Tom's intensity with a knife. These were during the preseason's earliest days, and he was already 100% locked in. He didn't dance. He didn't look left or right. He was stoic. Tom only stared at his office—the practice field—where he was about to conduct business for the next few hours, and that's precisely what he did, with the utmost precision and attention to detail.

When the practice started, it was Brady and not the coaches who got involved, ensuring players fully understood how to execute the drills correctly while reinforcing his expectations for their efforts and execution. From the time he started stretching that day until he walked off the field, Tom Brady was in total control because that was the standard he had set for himself and his team. Make no mistake, Bill Belichick was the head coach, but this was Brady's team in every way.

Tom was methodical and purposeful in everything he did, from overseeing drills to scrimmaging with the Redskins later on. The best part about this is that Tom not only brought his best game in what could have been a throwaway practice but also elevated his entire team and created a standard he expected them to meet.

When you step back and understand the degree to which Tom applied The Standard to his life, his accomplishments make much more sense. His dedication to maintaining his body through diet and ongoing workout routines is well documented. You can't reach peak performance without a mental component as well. Brady was as tough as nails, incorporating The Standard mindset into everything he did.

Brady is an extreme example of this philosophy. One thing is certain when fully immersing yourself in The Standard as a way of life. You can't turn off The Standard when you approach it correctly. After you succeed with this thinking, you don't want to either.

Just like Brady, it becomes so ingrained in your DNA that eventually, The Standard is the only way you know how to live. By the time I saw him up close in 2014, his work ethic and mindset had transcended to so many levels that he became the standard of winning. To this day, he remains the role model people from all walks of life point to when they want to "go for it," too.

Think about it. Brady, fueled by intense purpose, discipline, and desire, went from being a backup quarterback at Michigan who was drafted behind 198 other players in the 2000 NFL Draft to becoming the greatest quarterback ever to play the game. Ask yourself, "How was he able to do that?"

I visited the Patriots several times that season, and in every instance, the team's attitude and mindset were the same. Brady had instilled grit and determination at all levels of the organization.

The Standard carried the team through to Super Bowl XLIV. That day, I saw Tom throw for four touchdowns and engineer a 10-point fourth-quarter comeback to beat the Seahawks 28-24, giving Brady his fourth Super Bowl ring.

I got to celebrate with the team on the field afterward, which was the first time that season I saw Brady and his teammates joyfully cut loose. It was well deserved, but after a short celebration, they were already back at work figuring out what it would take to win another one.

Breaking it Down

Before applying The Standard to your life, you must understand precisely what it is. From there, you can start to implement and master the principles of The Standard as an overarching philosophy.

As a natural progression, you'll then be able to create a series of focused strategic and tactical standards to elevate specific parts of your life. You'll put your conscious and subconscious mind to work in areas where you want to improve, increasing your likelihood of success.

The first thing to understand about The Standard is that it is a simple concept. However, there are several individual elements you must also familiarize yourself with so that you can deeply embed The Standard into your way of thinking until it becomes second nature.

These elements are designed to work in unison and create the framework you will implement as a single, directed way of thinking. As you discover what they are and put them to work for you, some will be more important to you than others. Sometimes, that degree of importance will also shift from some elements to others, depending on your goals and motivation.

When applied correctly, the key is understanding that these elements will work in your favor for the desired outcomes.

To master The Standard philosophy, familiarize yourself with these elements and envision how to incorporate each into your life.

The Standard is meaningful. Pursuing something with all you've got makes no sense if you don't care enough about your goal. That sounds simple, but sometimes we set the bar high for ourselves just so we have something to aim at, which is a sure path to bad results. Be passionate about what you want to accomplish. Understand why you want to accomplish it. Your standard must not only be meaningful, but it should also mean everything to you.

The Standard is detailed. Implementing The Standard means implementing ways to measure your progress. The only way you do that is by setting up detailed processes at the beginning that are easy to track.

For example, don't just decide you want to lose weight. Decide that you want to lose thirty pounds over the next four months. Then build a more detailed action plan than "getting exercise" and "eating better." Your standard should be about going to the gym four times a week with a detailed workout plan and structuring your diet to include eating fifteen servings of vegetables, four meals of lean protein, and limiting your carbs as a starting point.

The Standard requires making the right choices. Suppose you start with a flawed premise or misinformation. In that case, you'll wind up with lesser results than if you did the hard work up front and made the right choices based on the best information available. Don't be so hurried that you bypass the initial structure and processes in favor of a quick win. The Standard does not work that way!

The Standard requires honesty and insightfulness. You hate it when others lie to you, so why would you lie to yourself? Nobody but you needs to know the truth, but you need to accept the truth and build that into elements of the standard you're going to create. Understand your limitations, weaknesses, and circumstances in your world as the basis of an honest starting point to create an achievable standard.

The Standard requires discipline. When you blend all the elements of The Standard, discipline should be much easier to incorporate. Properly armed with all the necessary tools creates the framework that leads to discipline to accomplish what you've set your sights on.

Early on, you may struggle with discipline, but as you get more in tune with your efforts and build repetition, discipline becomes a habit, and that habit creates a separate discipline standard. The key is not to give up or play loose and fast with your initial efforts. Flawed discipline produces flawed results.

The Standard eliminates motivation. Motivation is transient. It varies from moment to moment and from day to day. The Standard is constant. It is a set of principles you adhere to no matter how you feel. When you've set a standard of not eating sugary treats for the month, you eliminate the conflict of motivating yourself not to eat sweets. That decision has already been made, so you don't need to fight that battle.

The Standard answers "the why." One of the first questions you must ask when trying to lock in The Standard is, "Why do I want to do this?" This ties into honesty and a meaningful examination that will test your fortitude for what you want to accomplish. Suppose you can't immediately express the answer to this question. In that case, you need to spend more time to lock in a battle-hard response that becomes second nature over time.

The Standard challenges you to advance your life. Do stuff that matters! You can create all kinds of little standards that don't move the needle and fool yourself into thinking what you're doing to change your life is important. You should be a little unsure of the outcome when employing The Standard.

If you're a star high school pitcher, what good is it squaring off against twelve-year-olds in a little league game? Play up to your level of competition, and if you can, aim higher than that level if you want meaningful advances in your life. Standards should be challenging, with an element of risk and failure involved. You must live on the edge to go past the edge. Going past your edge is where you'll find your greatest rewards.

The Standard deletes negatives from your life. If you can use The Standard to eliminate bad things from your life, that is the equivalent of improving your life. Let's say you like to party hard on the weekends. At some point, you'll wake up feeling like crap, and heaven help you if you overindulge on a Sunday and you're expected to kick butt at your job on Monday. Eliminate or severely restrict getting hammered on Sunday, and you've eliminated a negative that helps propel the positives.

The Standard forces you to reflect on your core values. If you're under pressure to do things that don't conform to your values, you're going to be conflicted in your thoughts and actions. Some of that is unavoidable in all parts of your life. You need to pick and choose your battles, and sometimes they are imposed on you, like it or not.

However, you can use every experience like this to define who you are clearly, so when you do gain control of your life to a greater degree, you'll clearly understand the core values that define you. The other thing to remember is that you always have choices. The stakes may be high, but if you refuse to participate in something that crosses a line for you, you have found a meaningful standard you can bookmark and use in the future.

The Standard promotes ethical values. The world is a complicated place with endless choices that sometimes challenge who we are and what is important to us. You can apply passion to the standards you want to create, but you will be conflicted if there isn't a moral component to them.

For example, let's say you want to net $500,000 in earnings for the year. You'll have to fudge numbers, hide info from the IRS, close questionable deals, and do things that may be good for you but may hurt others. If you're thinking this way, you're in trouble. You're trading short-term successes for long-term peace of mind. It's dumb, unethical, and in many cases, could be illegal. Part of The Standard involves being a good human being at all times. Never violate this responsibility.

The Standard fulfills an emotional need without being emotional itself. By themselves, the standards you create are designed to be void of emotions. How you think and act is already predetermined. You do not need to endure the highs and lows of daily life in pursuit of your set standards. That's the beauty of The Standard. All the emotional haze is wiped away, and you're left with either doing or not doing in the clearest possible terms.

However, it's important to differentiate the standards you set versus why you want to accomplish them. Answering "the why" can be extremely emotional. It probably should be. Setting a standard of raising $1 million for cancer research is an ethical and noble pursuit. That emotional component can drive your efforts if you're doing it because your father died of cancer.

The Standard is your habits taken to the next level. Do not confuse your habits with your standards. Standards are more permanent than habits. Think of habits as the seeds you must plant that grow into standards. Habits are the small daily tasks you undertake that feed into the larger purpose that The Standard addresses. Think of The Standard as the parent and habits as the children, with both family members working to make your life better.

The Standard creates unreasonable and uncomfortable scenarios. You've already failed if you develop standards and are entirely comfortable with them from the outset. You want that uneasy feeling to be a part of the mix so that you'll feel an equally satisfying rush when you meet the standard you've set for yourself.

What good is it going to the gym because you've set the standard of getting stronger only to set a bench press goal of lifting 210 lbs. within three months when you're already pressing 200 lbs.? You're fooling yourself. Now apply that thinking if you set a goal of lifting 250 or 275 lbs. You are slightly more unsure of yourself with that goal. Don't be. Instead, frame it this way. If you set a goal of 275 lbs. and you only reach 260, how much better is your life than stopping after reaching a goal of only benching 210 lbs.?

Challenge yourself and be sure you're slightly uncomfortable when you do so. The bottom line is that The Standard is usually not pleasurable, but it is always compelling.

The Standard involves elements of risk. The only thing you need to remember about risk related to The Standard is that it's okay to fail. It's not okay not to try. The only caveat is that you shouldn't be comfortable with failure but understand that you will find outer limits because you're charting new places in your life. Outer limits are where the most risk resides and where the most growth occurs.

The Standard breeds confidence. There is something about a self-assured man or woman that attracts the forces of the world to them. When fully engaged with The Standard, you know exactly what you want and will or will not tolerate in your life. That degree of confidence helps you put your mind at ease and builds steppingstones to greater achievements. Confidence is like a magnet for similar-minded people. You will see the quality of your life and accomplishments rise significantly when you display more confidence.

The Standard grows self-esteem. It's critical to understand confidence, and self-esteem are not the same. Still, you will enjoy both as byproducts of The Standard. Confidence is outward facing. It's what you show the world. Self-esteem is connected to your inner self. It's what you show you. They work in tandem, and you typically can't have one without the other. However, they may reveal themselves at different times in your journey.

The Standard moves you closer to who *you* want to be. The Standard is personal. It is all about you and what you want to accomplish. So often, you've had to compromise who you are and want to be for the sake of others.

It started when you were a child and tried to please your parents. You did the same thing as a student for many years. And that often carries through as an adult in your relationship with your boss, spouse, and as part of your community. Combining these other obligations with The Standard can satisfy everyone in all parts of your life. It simply requires a shift in thinking that puts you more in charge of your life first. That's not selfish thinking. It's smart thinking.

The Standard is a public declaration. Although accountability is mainly internal, The Standard has a public and relational element. That can make your path easier since letting others know of your intentions can create allies to rally to your cause. You don't need to constantly remind people of your every move to support the standards you create, although many people do. Find the right level of public accountability for you, and then maintain a regular flow of updates and interim accomplishments to send messages to others in your sphere.

The Standard is unique to you but also sets an example for others. You become a role model by default with the right standards in place. How many children were inspired to elevate their game using Kobe Bryant's Mamba Mentality? Who among us doesn't dare to dream like Elon Musk? The world is full of high-achieving role models. This status is a secondary benefit that links to their primary missions. Still, many are happy to share their secrets to help others. If asked or you feel the need, you should too.

The Standard is not about being perfect. Get locked in on this. You are not perfect. You will never be perfect. Perfect does not exist. That is not meant to discourage you. It is meant to liberate you.

Relieved of the burden of perfection, you can go about your business in support of your standards the best way you know how. If you apply yourself diligently over time, you will progress toward the best version of yourself. Your effort can come close to perfect, which is the only way you should apply perfection to the outcomes you desire.

The Standard is not negotiable. With The Standard, either you do or you don't. There is no negotiation or compromise. It's so easy to slide here and there, which is antithetical to the most fundamental part of The Standard. When you sluff off your fudge efforts, you don't have standards in place. You only have habits that are still strong efforts that guide you correctly, but they are more immune to wiggle room than a rock-solid standard.

You may find some standards no longer serve you well. Instead of letting that nagging feeling stay with you for days and weeks, reexamine your core values, your "why," and other compelling reasons you chose that standard. Then recalibrate to create a new standard that better fits your current ambitions.

The Standard is all about consistency. When you employ The Standard philosophy in your life, the way you do one thing is the way you do everything. This is an insightful wisdom I learned from Coach Nick Saban while working with him. I have said this for years. The principles of The Standard should permeate all parts of your life. When you learn how to implement a standard in one part of your life, apply that lesson to as many parts of your life as possible. It removes directionless doubt, fear, and time-wasting activities. Consistency supports purpose, increases happiness, and leads to better-quality relationships.

The Standard is not about goals. Goals are based on reacting to external factors beyond your control. You don't have complete control of your external world, and that means your goals, while probably worthy, may not happen.

Shift your mindset from setting goals to creating standards. Standards are internal, and that means you can control them to a much higher degree. When you create a standard of putting in more hours at work (which you control), that gives you the best chance of reaching the goal of buying a nicer car or bigger home (which the outside world controls). Treat goals as byproducts instead of the primary driving force.

Now that you clearly understand what The Standard is, let's look closer at putting it to work for you.

CHAPTER 2

Implementing The STANDARD Philosophy

After you understand the elements that make up The Standard philosophy, you need a game plan to put them to work for you. Some of this requires creativity and a personalized approach on your part. You must make The Standard work in a way that makes the most sense to you. Not only must you own the elements, but you must own the process, too.

I've simplified that approach by creating the four Ps of The Standard Philosophy so you don't get too tied up in reams of minutia – **P**roblem, **P**lanning, **P**erformance, and **P**ayoff. Let me clarify. The Standard is all about creating an action plan instead of thinking about how to approach something, which often leads to procrastination. You prime the pump with many of the elements above. Still, ultimately, The Standard is about moving forward dynamically and purposefully.

To assist you in creating that actionable momentum, define the **Problem**, undertake thoughtful **Planning** as to how you'll create a standard, implement your **Performance**, and analyze the **Payoff**.

You can customize these steps according to your liking. Still, this process framework is the key to getting stuff done and improving your life.

The Problem

What problems do you want to solve? You already know where you're lacking and what you want to improve. Identifying the problem in broad strokes is not enough. You must be as specific as possible to ensure the best outcome.

For example, you're not simply overweight. You're fifty pounds overweight. That has created joint and back pain, low energy, depression, and many other issues that wrap themselves in your main problem.

Identifying the primary and secondary problems should naturally lead to why this problem matters to you. In this case, you could die early, hurting your family. Or this problem could generate new and more debilitating health issues later. It can also matter if your self-esteem and confidence have been torpedoed by being fat.

Don't gloss over this! Dig deep and get to the core of what's the problem.

The Planning

Ready, fire, and aim as a way of life is less than ideal. You must have a well-thought-out plan of attack that you can implement. Planning to overcome your problem should present some challenges for you. Overcoming those challenges is where the most growth occurs, so don't shy away from them. Embrace them instead.

If you're overweight, study nutrition, diet, wellness, exercise, mental health, and other related topics to be as educated as possible. Just don't do it endlessly at the expense of action.

Know what you can do, and then ask yourself, "How far beyond that you can go?" Make your planning process as detailed as possible to eliminate that fudge factor (pun intended!). Start thinking about desired outcomes based on the standard you set for losing weight. Things like lower cholesterol, reduced risk of diabetes, better heart health, better sleep, a more positive self-image, better mental health, and a dozen more outcomes should factor into how you attack the process.

The Performance

Do not endlessly make plans. Remember, perfection does not exist! At some point, even if your plan is evolving, you must dive in and move toward your desired outcomes. It's better to take imperfect action than to take no action, which will only maintain the status quo.

The great thing about The Standard is you can and should adjust based on gaining more knowledge or recognizing specific outcomes. Monitor, measure, and optimize to get what you want more effectively in less time and wasted motion.

The other thing is that you may be tempted to quit or ease up if you're not seeing the results you expected or no outward results. It sucks going to the gym for two weeks, hopping on the scale, and seeing you've only lost two pounds. There may be factors at work you're unaware of, but as long as your process is solid and your desire remains intact, you will see results. I guarantee it.

The Payoff

The payoff you get from implementing standards in your life will come to you in many ways. You'll notice a change in yourself. Others will notice a change in you.

The payoff is less of a celebration and more of a confirmation that you thought the right things and acted the right way based on what you want to achieve. If you want to pat yourself on the back for a job well done, I 100% encourage that but don't get caught in an ongoing celebration. You'll stumble and diminish what you just accomplished.

The payoff breeds a desire to keep doing more, applying elements of The Standard to other parts of your life. If you lost weight and are keeping it off, maybe now it's time to turn your attention to making more money in your career or working to improve your home life as a parent and spouse.

Armed with a philosophy that works for you, it's easy to execute The Standard to maximize your continued growth as you desire.

...

The Standard Philosophy is a framework that gives you the understanding and the tools you need to improve all parts of your life. With a firm grasp of The Standard elements, you can develop individual standards that address specific parts of your life. Expect overlap as you create standards in one part of your life because you have one life, and all parts are connected.

That is a natural benefit of implementing a single standard. You can use it as a building block to create multiple more targeted standards.

As you're about to read, I've used several standards in my work to produce incredible results for thousands of people over the years. All of them stem from The Standard philosophy as an overarching umbrella. You will see commonalities in the succeeding chapters, confirming how effective and flexible The Standard is in all situations.

If you're ready, turn the page, and you'll see dozens of examples of The Standard in action, which I've used to develop standards for almost twenty years.

The 4 P's of
THE STANDARD

#STANDARDoverFEELINGS #ATTACKthePROCESS

CHAPTER 3

Care Enough to Challenge Others, But...

Wat you're about to read may appear confusing at first. Still, it is one of the most important standards you can develop for yourself and your relationships with others. On the surface, you may first think it requires a balancing act, but once explained, no balancing act is required because the standard is absolute.

The standard I want you to consider is this.

To be successful when leading others, care enough to challenge them but put the standards you've developed above your feelings.

As you read in the first chapter, The Standard fulfills an emotional need without being emotional itself. In the purest form, your standards should be void of emotions. We're all born with emotions in the real world, and learning to control those emotions is a lifelong challenge at which we often fail. The more intense the situation, the more we attach strong emotions to it, which often affects how we decide on a course of action. As a result, when things don't go as planned, we get angry and frustrated, and many of us sulk for days or weeks, lamenting the outcome and drowning in depression.

The confusing part in developing a standard that addresses how we deal with our emotions is that one size does not fit all. Every person and every situation is different. What triggers you one way will not trigger you the same way when something else with an emotional element attached to it takes place.

You're human, meaning you will always have emotions to work through. In that way, when dealing with others, you will attach emotions to people and events, like it or not. The key, and the lesson you need to learn, is that you need to separate the emotions that give an undertaking value for you and subjugate them to standards that you should also have in place to help you think things through clearly and logically.

The standard you create for particular situations is a blend of many components. Still, the most important of these is having contingencies in place that account for the emotions you and others will experience. The "why" can be emotional. In fact, it is often preferable. But your standard needs to take the pole position over any feelings you have when trying to accomplish the tasks.

The John Qualy Question

Many years ago, I learned the importance of caring enough to challenge others but still put a standard above feelings.

In 2006, I was a financial advisor working for a Fortune 100 company. I had hit an extended rough patch where nothing was going right. I wasn't setting enough quality appointments, and I couldn't close deals to save my life. On top of that, some things at the corporate level were also unsettling. Over time, that frustration grew, and I could slowly feel my blood boiling a little more with each setback that, under normal circumstances, wouldn't have phased me at all.

One day, I reached my limit. Filled with a fair amount of anger and frustration, I scheduled an hour-long meeting with my managing partner, John Qualy. John is not only one of the greatest leaders I have ever known, but he is also a mentor and remains a second father to me.

I walked into his office and was so upset I don't even remember how the conversation started. I let all my emotions cut loose and launched into a tirade for three minutes straight. To his credit, John sat there and stoically let me unload on him. Like all people who carry around strong emotions, getting it out helped a lot, and eventually, I took a breath and calmed down.

John took a deep breath and waited for one or two beats to see if I would fire off again. Seeing I was played out from my opening salvo, he slowly and deliberately moved his glasses to the bridge of his nose and looked me straight in the eyes.

Then he changed the entire tone of the conversation with one simple question, "What would your mother want you to do right now?"

Those who know me and my work will understand why that question was so important to me. For those who don't, a brief explanation is in order.

Some people, like John and many others, lead hundreds or thousands of people and have the power to impact lives through their thoughts and actions. Others only impact one or two lives, but if one of those people is you, that can have more significance when those impactful people are an intimate part of your life. That was the case with my mother, Janet Fishman Newman.

Although she passed away at an early age many years ago, she was a strong force in my life, setting an example of how to stay connected to her reason to live as a way to get the most out of every day. I have since turned this into what I now call The Burn. It is one of my core peak performance pillars that I have written about extensively and is also the name of my weekly podcast.

Despite a fatal diagnosis of amyloidosis, she never wavered in her love for us. Taking care of me and my brother Drew in any way she could become an unwavering standard that stayed with her until the day she died. She overcame incredible pain and remained in our lives for as long as she could, but my mother also taught me one of the most important concepts of following The Standard as a basis for your life.

John knew this story, and with that one question, he brought me back to the most personal reason I have for following standards-based life. After ranting for three minutes, which could have easily gone on for the entire hour I had scheduled, John brought me back to reality in under ten seconds. He completely understood the expectancy theory, which posits that what you focus on expands.

Focusing on the positive gives you more positives in your life. When you focus on the negative, you get more negatives in your life.

John's question was a reset that brought me back to a positive mindset and destroyed the negativity that had dominated me for several weeks. It was brilliant on his part and a great example of his leadership and activating the right standard at the right time.

Ultimately, we both got what we wanted. John got back fifty-seven minutes of his life, and I got a huge reminder of the standard my mother had taught me. Using that, I had no trouble jumping up with a renewed purpose to make phone calls and put my negativity behind me.

John cared about me as a friend and an employee. Still, he also knew both of us needed to put the standard of positivity front and center instead of giving in to the negative and temporary feelings I was going through. John understood what my Burn was and then fortified it by asking me a question and allowing me to uncover and take ownership of my behavior instead of lecturing and hoping for the best.

Putting The Standard Over Feelings

You should care enough to challenge others, but the key still demands that those people rise to a standard, overcoming feelings that could undermine a desired outcome. If you want success in your life and successful outcomes in others you lead, manage, or care about, understanding this concept is essential.

Another of my favorite examples of putting a standard over feelings involves Claudio Gambin, one of my longtime coaching clients. When I met him several years ago, he was an ambitious financial advisor, still early in his career. Although he was already a high-producing wealth manager, he wanted to do better than his $700,000 annual sales.

Shortly after I started coaching him, we were in Orlando, driving to a dinner meeting, and I asked him pointedly, "What is it that makes you great?" I specifically wanted to know what connected him to his Burn so that I could tap into that as a way to grow his bottom-line productivity and wealth.

As he started to answer, he quickly grew emotional. The daily efforts that formed his work standard were fueled by his parents' sacrifice. Claudio's parents came to the United States in search of a better life for their children, leaving behind incredible jobs in Brazil to build a better life for Claudio and his sister. They left behind a good life and traded that in to work multiple jobs to provide better opportunities for the children they loved so dearly.

Claudio was touched deeply by their sacrifices, and he became motivated to make sure their efforts were not in vain. I helped him strengthen the connection between his Burn to The Standard.

While his work ethic was already outstanding, he used his feelings of loyalty and love for his parents and what they had done for him to create an unwavering standard that honored their sacrifices. He became even more disciplined and vowed never to feel guilt for not giving his best every day. His standard meant showing up and doing the hard work to drive his success, knowing those feelings for his parents were important but that creating the right standard was even more important to the outcomes he wanted.

Fast forward to today. Using his feelings as the basis to create and enhance a standard, Claudio now generates more than $13 million annually in revenue.

Another story exemplifies caring enough to challenge others but developing a standard that supersedes those feelings for the best outcome. It involves a person many of you already know, Coach Nick Saban, and the standard he created with the Alabama football program.

I worked as the Crimson Tide's mental conditioning coach for five years, and I could pick from hundreds of examples of the standard that Coach Saban instilled from top to bottom as part of the program. However, there is one small example involving Jalen Hurts that reveals the entire mindset of the program. It demonstrates how each player, coach, and everyone connected to the program must put aside feelings in favor of that standard.

Jalen Hurts is arguably one of the most talented athletes to ever play under Coach Saban. He demonstrated that talent in college and, more recently, as a quarterback who took his team to Super Bowl LVII, where the Eagles came up a little short against Patrick Mahomes and the Kansas City Chiefs in a 38-35 nail-biter.

I firmly believe the standard Coach Saban instilled in him at Alabama is a big reason for his ongoing success as one of the best quarterbacks in the NFL. I could write reams about the standard and the culture at Alabama. Still, it's easily condensed into this one small act that tells you everything about putting a standard above feelings.

Alabama played and beat Georgia in the 2018 national championship game. Jalen had a subpar performance in the first half. He was benched in the second half in favor of freshman Tua Tagovailoa who closed out the 35-28 victory.

The following season, Jalen and Tua battled it out in training camp to determine who would be the starting quarterback for the Crimson Tide. It was a tough battle between the two, but Tagovailoa eventually prevailed. When I showed up for one of my sessions after the fourth week of the season, the team was 4-0 and ranked first in the country. By then, Jalen had already made it known that he would transfer to another program at the end of the season. He eventually moved after settling on the University of Oklahoma for his final year of eligibility.

A decision of that magnitude is difficult, and you can be sure Jalen poured a lot of feelings and emotions into making it. You might also expect after making that decision that Jalen would immediately check out while riding the bench and thinking about what next season would bring. You would be wrong.

Jalen set his feelings aside and displayed leadership and a standard instilled in him as part of the Alabama program. Here's how I know that for a fact. During my visit, I walked into the weight room. One freshman had shown up late for a strength and conditioning session, and he was directed to push a plate around the weight room to drill into him the importance of being on time and ready to work every day. When he finished his penance, one of the strength coaches approached him and launched into a lecture about the Alabama standard and why his behavior was unacceptable.

Before he could get more than a couple of sentences out, Jalen walked across the weight room and tapped the strength coach on the shoulder to let him know he would handle the situation with the freshman. For the next several minutes, I watched Jalen Hurts, a man who knew he was leaving the program at the end of the season, quietly and firmly counsel that freshman on the Alabama standard and the expectations that all were required to follow.

Jalen set aside his emotions at being benched and rose to the level of the standard that had been instilled in him and reinforced that standard in a way that only another player could.

Why did Jalen Hurts do that? Because it had been hard-wired into his football DNA as part of the Alabama program. Jalen had learned a valuable lesson that living by The Standard means that while you can have feelings and also care enough to challenge others, ultimately, it is the standard that stays with you when those feelings go away, which eventually they always do.

CHAPTER 4

Don't Trust the Process

The adage "trust the process" has been used in coaching circles a lot in recent years, but various forms of the same kind of thinking have been around much longer than that.

It's a good notion but doesn't address the issue of doing everything possible to get the desired results. In that way, "trust the process" is flawed thinking, and my advice to you is not to trust the process. I want you to aim higher.

I want you to **Attack the Process** as your standard in life.

Here's the difference. Simply trusting the process cedes too much control to forces beyond your peak capabilities. Trust has an element of faith attached to it, and while you need faith to do great things, you need a lot more than that. Trust also implies that the faith you have will also lead to finding peace as well.

For many people, that's enough. In practical terms, trust also tells your brain that everything will eventually work out in your favor if you follow all the elements of your process. Mentally, it gives you an out, subconsciously telling your brain you can ease up on the gas because unseen forces will aid you when you need them the most. It's nice to think that will be the case more often than not, but in reality, unless you apply every bit of your skills, talents, and abilities to a problem, there's a much higher probability that your efforts won't break in your favor as often as they could.

You need to have a well-thought-out process. However, that process should include an aggressive element to it. Think of it as a warrior mentality, if you must. You are going into battle with unseen forces aligned against you. Not in a direct way but in a competitive environment, whether you're doing business in a boardroom, on a court, on a field, or in almost every other part of your life.

I've had zero problems with developing that process. It's critical to your success. Putting trust in the process is vague, and to my way of thinking, placing faith in your process gives you a much easier out when the process falls short.

Ask yourself if trust is enough to carry the day. Or do you want to develop a standard that is more aggressive and gives you an added edge? Trusting the process is good. Attacking the process is head and shoulders better when you're setting a standard for yourself. In a world that has often become cutthroat and echoing a philosophy to win at all costs, you can still maintain your decorum. However, I also think trusting the process is no longer enough in such times. Instead, you must attack the process to elevate your standard and results.

Developing an Attack the Process Standard

I recognized the need to attack the process many years ago. Seeing how quickly the world was moving and how complex it had become, I knew that an action-oriented process was the key to succeeding against growing pressures and odds often stacked against people.

To maintain consistent results by focusing on daily activities instead of trying to control outcomes beyond our control, I developed the Prizefighter Day standard. It is a detailed action plan that, at its core, is an Attack the Process standard. By shifting to activities, you can control instead of focusing on results you cannot; the Prizefighter Day standard gives you the best chance of throwing knockout punches against obstacles, pressures, and anxieties that can overwhelm you much of the time.

The Prizefighter Day works like this.

Identify activity-driven daily disciplines you can control in your life. For example, if you want to lose twenty pounds, you know you can get there with the proper diet and exercise. You will lose twenty pounds over time when you attack the process by eating the right foods and building in fat-burning exercises. You will eventually reach your goal by focusing on those activities instead of the outcome.

The key to any standard is to be consistent. In this case, if you eat the right foods every day and exercise diligently several times a week, those standards will propel you to the desired outcome.

To bring balance to people's lives, I often encourage them to create YOUR Prizefighter Day in these three areas:

Personal. Find a discipline that is just for you. That may be waking up early every morning and reading the *Bible* to improve your spiritual health, working out, meditating, or taking your dogs for a walk to achieve the goal of less stress in your life.

Professional. Set a specific discipline for the number of phone calls, emails, and sales volume you want to achieve in your daily business efforts. This is critical to creating an income-enhancing and job-satisfaction ripple effect.

Service to others. Reach out to others struggling or needing a kind word to help them through their day. There is no more important standard than spending time with others in need, and you should use this as the opportunity to grow your soul while practicing care for others.

Make it a point to accomplish these actions as early in the day as possible. Remember that these are not results you can't control. These behaviors enhance and reinforce the other parts of your life, and the best part is they are easy to do when you make them a non-negotiable part of your morning. You immediately create a daily sense of accomplishment that leads to a balanced and more rewarding life, personally and professionally.

Essentially, when you create your Prizefighter Day, you are also building out your ideal morning and putting yourself on a path to perform, regardless of any obstacles and challenges that come your way.

The keys to building an appropriate Prizefighter Day are defining the right goals and consistency, which should be challenging but achievable. You must do the actions you've committed to each day. Do not be swayed into complacency when you enjoy some success, either.

The Attack the Process standard is a long-term strategy that produces tremendous results over months and years. You must attack the process and accomplish them one day at a time with strategies such as Prizefighter Day.

Tom Izzo Attacks the Process

In 1998, I started attending Michigan State University as one of the thousands of wide-eyed freshmen who descend on the campus each school year. I was fired up like you wouldn't believe, knowing I was attending the same campus where one of my heroes, Magic Johnson, had left an incredible legacy. Initially, I wanted to attend Missouri, but my dad nixed the idea because he thought it was too much of a party school. He had doubts that I'd be able to stay focused on getting my education. In hindsight, he may have been right!

My dad didn't know that MSU was an even more notorious party school up north of my home in suburban St. Louis. I somehow forgot to mention that fact to him after being shut out of Missouri as a destination.

I didn't know it then, but my first year on the MSU campus coincided with the start of one of the most incredible runs in college basketball history. That run, and my pure joy at being a Spartan, were two seeds planted that year and laid the foundation for my work later on with the Michigan State basketball and football programs.

The 1998 basketball season began Tom Izzo's winning run as the Spartan's basketball coach. In his first season, winning the Big Ten championship in 1998, they put together a 33-5 record, going up against conference powerhouses like Wisconsin and Illinois before putting together an NCAA tournament run that included beating Kentucky before losing to Duke in the Final Four.

I was at the game against Purdue when the Spartans clinched the Big Ten Championship. Being a spirited freshman, I was one of the hundreds who stormed the court at the Breslin Center. As fate would have it, I eventually found myself face to face with Coach Izzo, and without thinking, I gave him a big hug. Of course, he had no idea who I was, and with the way security has changed, I doubt my first meeting with Coach Izzo would have any shot of taking place that way today.

Before I ever came close to hugging Coach Izzo, I was no stranger to basketball, having played for Ladue High School. I wasn't the most talented player on the team, but even then, I was the most motivated.

In fact, I showed so much hustle, determination, and heart that Coach Todd Basler named me team captain. If I'm being honest, I was slow-footed and had a hard time playing defense against all the other speedsters on the court, but I did log minutes because I had a great long-range jumper. Slow-footed but with a great shot wasn't precisely a lethal combination that made opponents fear me. I attracted attention from Division III programs before realizing I'd be better off hanging up my high tops and investing earnestly in my education.

Everything indeed happens for a reason. In this case, part of that reason was so I could have a front-row seat for the start of Coach Izzo's incredible run at Michigan State, including a National Championship in the 2000 season. Coach Izzo's teams became known for their heart, discipline, and physicality, giving them the edge every time they stepped on the court. What I watched repeatedly as a student was a locked-in standard that, at its core, was all about attacking the process. Coach Izzo exploited that edge and won hundreds of games using it to lead the Spartans to eight Final Four appearances in his 28 years at Michigan State. However, the more impressive accomplishment occurred in 2023. Coach Izzo became the first coach ever to reach twenty-five straight NCAA tournaments.

The Attack the Process standard also had another positive effect. The top players in the country who saw Coach Izzo's standard and the results it produced quickly gravitated to the program. The standard created an upward spiral that attracted the best of the best during his tenure there. As it turns out, years after I gave him that hug on the court, I was one of those people who became a part of the program as well.

After putting together a track record as a peak performance and mental conditioning coach and at the urging of several former Spartan players, Coach Izzo and I reconnected. I started doing "secret sauce" videos to infuse passion for players who wanted to attack their next level of talent and greatness. I did this for several Final Four runs. Still, it wasn't until the 2022-23 season that I could enter the locker room and speak to players in person. It's one thing to create videos but quite another to build a personal relationship with players to help them reach their goals.

What attracted me to the program as a college freshman was still as strong as ever twenty-five years later. From the moment I entered the Spartan facility, I could feel The Standard was deeply encoded into the Spartan's DNA. There were certain expectations about thinking, practicing, and stepping on the court to play the Spartan brand of basketball. The process worked, and even though opponents had dissected every part of the MSU program, the standard was so high that they couldn't derail it, even with the mindset and game plan in hand.

As an alumnus, a mental conditioning coach, a fan of Coach Izzo and the Spartan program, and now armed with a complete understanding of the importance of The Standard, I quickly saw all the elements I've talked about in play during my locker room visits.

It permeated everything from coaching players one-on-one to team practices to how the team conducted itself 24/7.

The level of success Coach Izzo produced for over twenty-five years was characterized by no compromise, no letdowns, no excuses, and not allowing anything less than players bringing their best to the court every time.

Another thing worth noting is that Coach Izzo's standards and influence spread far beyond the basketball program. It was so significant that the new campus *football* complex is called the Tom Izzo Football Building.

Speaking of MSU football, I have also worked with the Spartan football program. I can readily see Coach Izzo's influence on head football coach Mel Tucker. That's one of the best things about the Attack the Process standard. It's portable and teachable.

My working relationship with Coach Tucker has morphed into one of the closest relationships I have personally and professionally. When my father passed away, Coach Tucker was not only one of the first people to call and offer his condolences, but he was also ready to fly to St. Louis and spend time with me to help me heal from my loss.

He not only exemplifies what it means to attack the process, but he has also brought his version of that standard to the MSU football program and his personal life. He has earned every bit of success in his twenty-six-year coaching career as a part of college football championship teams and as an NFL coach for ten years.

Coach Tucker takes care of the Xs and Os as well as anyone, but what makes his success special is his attention to detail and his ability to build relationships with his players, coaches, and everyone connected to the program.

There's no more high-profile example of why that's important than how he and Coach Izzo reacted after February 13, 2023. On that date, a deranged shooter stalked victims on the MSU campus, killing three people and wounding five others. It was a tragic episode in every sense of the word. While you can't change what happened, you can be a strong visible force for calm and healing in the aftermath, which is what both coaches did.

They used their investments in their campus community to help the entire city of East Lansing and beyond get past the initial shock and long-term heartbreak that would hang over that campus for years. Through their love and passion and how much they had invested in their programs, fans, the student body, and the city itself, Coach Izzo and Coach Tucker brought a standard of healing to a community collectively wounded by this heinous act. That was one of the unintended but positive consequences on display by living life to The Standard.

The bottom line is this. Don't simply trust the process. That is no longer enough. Instead, set an Attack the Process standard to create your life's biggest and best wins.

CHAPTER 5

The Requirements of the Unrequired

I f you want to enjoy some degree of success in life, there are specific required standards that you must meet to reach that threshold. Those are the standards required of you daily to win.

However, suppose you're driven to achieve more. In that case, you must elevate your efforts to create an Unrequired Standard. With this mindset, your winning efforts won't be good enough. Instead, you'll need to rise to the next level with added discipline and accountability. Part of how you'll do this is to cultivate a close relationship with a mentor or performance coach and aggressively let those around you know you're hungry for more success. Send a clear message to everyone that you're actively seeking to advance in your company or industry. That will give you a solid foundation to take the next steps to become a high performer who taps into the Unrequired Standard.

The Unrequired Standard means doing the things other people can't see, won't do, or talk about. Implementing this mindset involves making those things a priority. The key to the Unrequired Standard is understanding that you can't activate unrequired activities until you have accomplished your required standards.

To move into the unrequired thoughts and actions, you must silence the seduction of success. The Unrequired Standard demands that you commit fully to the next level, where many people won't go, and you can only do that when you eliminate distractions, including whatever level of success you've already achieved. You must become obsessed with attacking that next level and stacking it on top of your required standard activities already in place.

Few people have that level of desire. Not everyone will pay that price. You must look in the mirror long and decide if you are serious about leading an uncommon life. If the answer is yes, then part of that answer will include framing added unrequired disciplines as opportunities to help you reach your goals instead of challenges that you must undertake with a high cost attached to them. When you're willing to frame that next level the right way, you're well on your way to meeting the Unrequired Standard.

In a more detailed form, the Unrequired Standard means showing up earlier, putting in more reps, making more phone calls, and devoting more hours to your goal. Simply put, you must have a hardcore desire to outwork your competition or dig even deeper to overcome barriers standing in your way. Pay close attention to weighing risk and time spent vs. the rewards your added actions will produce. Your time is at an even higher premium than before, so you must unmercifully calculate and evaluate the returns against the commitment you will make. This attention to detail and laser focus isn't for everyone. However, if you're reading this book, there's a good chance the Unrequired Standard is for you.

Like all standards, the Unrequired Standard may start with desire. Still, until you thoughtfully decide what you want to do and how far you want to go, and then take the specific and directed actions to put you closer, you're just playing mind games with yourself.

The Unrequired Standard is not something where you flip a switch and are on your way. It combines reverse engineering in great detail with what you've done in the past. You must fully understand what has worked best to help you get to where you are thus far. Then you must supersize those efforts and add new, efficient, and dynamic actions to complement your current situation. For example, if you have your best success calling on clients on Tuesday or Wednesday, start an hour earlier, put in two hours later, limit your unnecessary chatter with team members, stay off social media, and drive intentional focus on what matters most. That extra effort elevates you to a new level when combined with what you're already doing.

Soon enough, doing these unrequired actions will pay dividends. It may take thirty days. It may take six months. In some cases, it may take several years. The simple fact is that when you make the added effort and do targeted high-value activities consistently with discipline over time, you put yourself in a better place to get the desired results.

Are these results guaranteed? Hell, no! Anyone who tells you success is guaranteed is blowing smoke at you. You can't control the outcome. However, you can heavily influence those results by doing the unrequired actions that others won't do.

You should incorporate new unrequired activities gradually. There is no need to go from zero to 100 miles per hour at the start. Don't do it. You need to rack up small and incremental victories that help you build momentum and test what you believe are the most effective unrequired activities. Your efforts should be challenging. In other words, don't complete an extra thirty minutes of work a week and feel good about your efforts. You're conning yourself, and that's nothing more than a waste of time. Conversely, you do not need to overwhelm yourself with massive additions that put too much pressure on you, possibly leading to failure from reaching too high. Smart, sensible, and high-return activities are the key.

While developing the Unrequired Standard mindset, you create short-term habits that will change and layer into your existing efforts. Your unrequired efforts must be challenging but achievable. Remember, you are already working to a required standard that must be challenging in its own way. Chances are, you already have a relatively high activity level, producing results for you. The key is efficiently finding the next level most others won't go to and exploiting that difference. When you add these unrequired activities, they will compound. For example, if you want to add more muscle to your arms, doing two extra sets of bicep curls in the gym three times a week translates into over three hundred extra sets yearly. Maybe you're a marathon runner. If you build stamina by running fifty miles a week, how much faster will your time be if you run sixty or seventy miles a week instead? Over time, the math always works in your favor.

Developing an Unrequired Standard also requires you to make it a priority. Now is the time to be obsessive with a long-term game in mind. Get creative in prioritizing how you spend your time and build your environment to drive accountability. Eliminate as many distractions as possible.

Committing to an Unrequired Standard is not for everybody. This thinking forces you to decide how badly you want to go to the next level, where few people dare to live. As you'll see below, the payoffs can be well worth the effort.

Fostering Wealth with the Unrequired Standard

Foster Victor Wealth Advisors in Greenville, South Carolina, is one of my long-standing coaching clients. I attend their annual planning meeting and work with them yearly to drive accountability and growth. At one of these planning meetings in 2017, we held a roundtable discussion about goals for the coming year.

They were a fairly small firm. While they had already achieved sizable results, managing more than a half billion dollars in funds, they aggressively sought to grow that number. Initially, they set $80 million in new assets under management for 2017. That was a solid and challenging target, given they only had five advisors. However, in my mind, that was a "required goal" if they wanted healthy growth. However, I wanted to push them and see if they were serious about blasting through that amount to something even bigger. I rarely accept the first answer I hear in situations like this.

So, I asked them, "You know, $80 million is close to $100 million under management. Are you up for aiming for $100 million instead?"

The room grew quiet. Then one of them blurted out, "We've never even done $80 million, and now you want us to aim for another $20 million over and above that?"

"Yes," I said calmly. Collectively, they had already written their dollar goals for the year.

I coached them on what it meant to implement the Unrequired Standard by challenging them to think bigger and contemplate new ways to attack those larger goals. In other words, what unrequired efforts could they make to ensure a bigger bottom-line number? Then I had them toss that group exercise aside and told them to individually write what they wanted to achieve as a dollar goal instead.

When they were done, I had them read their individual goals but with an Unrequired Standard now folded into the process. Stripped away from the safety of only doing what they had done to produce a certain level of results in the past, they took on this new challenge fortified by the belief that they could do more. They leaned into it without reserve.

As they read their individual goals, I stood at the whiteboard and tallied the numbers. Bolstered by an Unrequired Standard mindset, that new goal for the year was now $110 million.

On the outside, I gave them a little smile. On the inside, I was fired up! They listened. They reacted. They believed they could accomplish something bigger.

The rest of the planning session involved reconfirming their existing efforts and adding an unrequired overlay. What was that overlay? It was pretty simple. They agreed to contact two additional A++ contacts every day. There was no pressure to schedule appointments or push hard to close deals because those are often beyond their control. When leaving that meeting, I knew the simple act of adding a small number of contact actions, compounded over an entire year, would produce results. If they were diligent, the deals would happen. In subsequent follow-ups, I reinforced those unrequired actions to create accountability and focus, tying it to the firm's core productivity message.

Fast forward to a year later. It's January 2018, and I'm dying to know what the final tally for the year was. Paul Foster, one of the firm's founders whom I was close to by working together as financial advisors at Northwestern Mutual, sent me an email with a spreadsheet as we hopped on a call to let me know how the year turned out.

I opened the spreadsheet, and Paul told me to focus on two numbers. "Our goal was $110 million for the year, and quite frankly, I wondered how we would get there. Now scroll over to that number at the bottom on the far right," he said.

That's when I saw the figure of $118 million under management. It was a rush I'll never forget. However, there was another number that was just as important. Paul also had me scroll to the far right in his tracking column. As part of our planning a year earlier, I had challenged him personally to do $42 million for the year. I thought it was essential for him to set the pace as a founder and team leader. I was ecstatic when I saw his total for 2017 was $60 million!

Paul clarified he focused on consistency and never missed his unrequired targets for the year. He was also clear in letting me know he focused on the baseline required work first. Otherwise, the Unrequired Standard would have no meaning.

As I've stated, the Unrequired Standard isn't some big hairy audacious thing you must add to your already full plate of things to do. Its beauty lies in taking your hard work and doing just a little more. You've heard the saying, "It's a game of inches." That's really what the Unrequired Standard is all about—moving the ball just a few extra inches daily until you cross the goal line. That is how the highest performers out gun, out-hustle, and win more often than everyone else. They live and breathe the Four Ps and refuse to be seduced by a level of success from only doing the required.

Those are the requirements of the Unrequired Standard. They work and have been proven dozens of times in my personal experience and untold times on a larger scale among peak performers in all professions, businesses, sports, and more.

There is one other number worth noting from this story. Foster Victor Wealth Advisors has used the Unrequired Standard every year since we first implemented it.

In our 2023 planning session, Paul Foster proudly revealed that they have almost $1.5 billion of assets under management.

CHAPTER 6

The Duality of Aggressive Patience

At first blush, the notion that you can be aggressive and patient simultaneously doesn't seem possible. Being aggressive is an attack-oriented action. Patience is a thoughtful, reserved state of mind where actions are minimal or non-existent. In their ways, both are products of mental toughness and intentional effort. Both are also paths to successful outcomes, and those commonalities indicate how they can be married to each other. The question remains. How is it possible to link these seemingly opposite strategies to create a standard of Aggressive Patience?

Like many other standards, Aggressive Patience is a product of discipline and consistency. You must take a long-term approach and be willing to pay the price by not losing sight of your goal, which may take months or years to accomplish.

One of the best examples I can cite involves how I approached my career, starting as a financial advisor. I was in that industry for ten years, but it took me a while to learn what I needed to and decide early on that I wanted to be one of the industry's top producers. In fact, during my first training class in 2004, I told the trainer that I would become part of Northwestern Mutual's Forum, which was reserved as an honor for the top 1% of producers out of the company's 10,000 advisors. It was partly cocky and confident on my part but also a challenging and worthy goal that I could only reach if I built the standards and habits I needed to succeed.

I did everything I could in my first year as an advisor to hit that target. I was aggressive, like few people had seen. If you know anything about the financial services business, you know it takes years to build and grow your client base. So, as you may guess, I fell way short of my goal.

However, I laid the right groundwork and consistently put in the work to finish in the top five in the country for *new* advisors with less than four years of experience, which was an incredibly remarkable result for someone completely new to the industry. Others were impressed and took notice, asking me to speak about how I succeeded as a newcomer. As it turns out, those were the first seeds planted for what would become my calling later in life.

I was happy with the results. However, I still hadn't reached my 1% goal. During that time, I figured out it might take a while to climb to the top of the mountain. I didn't know how long, but I knew I had the proper framework. That way, I became aggressively patient and created a foundational standard that makes many other things possible.

I publicly restated my goal at the start of my second year in the business. That second year came and went, and although I continued to make great strides, I fell woefully short of my Forum goal again. The same thing happened in my third year as well, but I made progress along the way, gaining recognition as a financial advisor who was a top-five producer in their first four years in the business. It was a nice but qualified accolade and not the ultimate goal I wanted. I continued to work hard and bide my time. I believed in what I was doing, so the aggressive patient climb up the mountain got easier. I did not change my goal, let doubt creep in, or weaken my mindset.

In my fourth year as a financial advisor, it happened. As a producer, I moved into the top 1% of the company and became a Northwestern Mutual Forum member. Although it took me four years, that short timeframe was unheard of and brought me financial security and industry notoriety. I owe it all to the duality of aggressive patience.

I continued to be a top producer for the next several years. I became an in-demand speaker at company gatherings, industry forums, and other events based on my accomplishments.

As you can guess, because I didn't give up, the Aggressive Patience Standard led me to make the unheard-of career change out of the financial services industry and into a peak performance coaching and speaking career.

The Stonecutters Credo

The world of college football is a generally unforgiving place. I can easily argue that it is more competitive than professional football because players are only at their schools for four years or fewer, the fans are more rabid, wealthy alums can add a difficult overlay, and players often play for that golden ticket into the NFL.

At the center of all of this is the program's head coach. While everyone wants to win and win now, there are dozens of competing interests that a wise coach and their staff must constantly juggle. If you want a peek inside one of the most intense forms of aggressive patience, take note of what goes on in any college football program. The same holds for all college athletic programs, but I think it's the most intense with football.

I could pick and choose from several programs to help explain the Aggressive Patience Standard, but I wanted to tell you about Coach Chris Klieman. He became a coaching legend at North Dakota State before taking the head coaching job at Kansas State in 2019. By the end of the 2022 season, his combined coaching record was 102-33, and his Bison teams had won four FCS championships during his five seasons as head coach at North Dakota State (in 2015, I became his performance coach at NDSU). His transition to head coach at Kansas State makes him eminently qualified as an example of the Aggressive Patience Standard.

That part of his story started on the eve of prepping his Bison team for their national championship game against Eastern Washington at the end of the 2018 season. Coach Klieman had already accepted the K State job for the following season, but his only condition was that he must be allowed to finish the season at North Dakota State. He could have walked away from the program in the season with nothing left to prove, but that loyalty was a form of patience he displayed to finish his tenure the right way. He had to deal with the competing interest of moving on, but he did so with class and loyalty to the entire Bison program.

The team had gone undefeated during the regular season and beat Montana State, Colgate, and South Dakota State to advance to the championship game against Eastern Washington, winning 38-24 to complete a 15-0 season.

While simultaneously preparing for those post-season games, Coach Klieman was already thinking about how he would transition to his new coaching position. He was entering a program wrapping up a challenging 5-7 season, which was unacceptable to the abovementioned groups.

Coach Klieman and I started talking about how we would build a winning culture, knowing where he wanted to go was not happening in a single season. He was facing an uphill battle with recruiting, and players were wary about coming to K-State because they perceived the program was far behind others in the Big 12 Conference. Coach Klieman was also replacing the legendary Bill Snyder, who had racked up many awards as head coach. Facing a challenging environment like this, it quickly became apparent that an aggressive patience mindset would be required over multiple seasons.

I was reading a book called *Pound the Stone* by Joshua Medcalf, and one theory he espoused was embracing the Stonecutter's Credo. It was first put forth by Jacob Riis, a poor Danish immigrant who ultimately became a police reporter for the New York Tribune in the late 1800s. His thinking and writing were simple and brilliant and the perfect summation of the Aggressive Patience Standard.

> *When nothing seems to help, I look at a stonecutter hammering away at his rock perhaps a hundred times without as much as a crack showing in it. Yet at the hundred and first blow, it will split in two, and I know it was not that blow that did it, but all that had gone before.*

I explained the credo to him and the necessity of pounding the stone one day at a time to put in the work that greatness requires. We both knew that putting a standard like this in place and focusing on the process instead of results was the path to winning over the long term. In addition, to overcome some headwinds we were facing, another critical element involved instilling the power of more belief, both in the program and in each coach and player associated with the program.

From this, the goals we put in place were further bolstered as we aggressively got everyone to buy into putting forth their best effort every day, knowing effort and mindset were things we could control to reach those goals. Rather than speak and activate these things into existence, I also created a laminated bookmark with bold "POUND THE STONE" lettering on one side and the program's goals on the other side. That added reinforcement was part of an overall plan to constantly remind everyone associated with the program of what we were trying to accomplish and the mindset we would use to make it happen.

Against this backdrop, we also knew transforming a college football program doesn't take place overnight, so we also understood we would need to remain patient and give a new culture time to mature and bear fruit.

We set several first-year goals, including going 8-5 and getting invited to a bowl game. Coach Klieman pounded that stone hard every day, and at the end of the season, his team won eight games and was invited to the Liberty Bowl. Buoyed by that success, the next level goal was to win a Big 12 Championship by the 2021 season. Unfortunately, the COVID pandemic turned things upside down and put a big fat asterisk on that college football season, so our next-level conference championship goal was a bit delayed. Coach Klieman used that time to keep working patiently toward the program's championship goal. In the third year of the Pound the Stone era, the program took a huge stride, beating a powerhouse SEC opponent, LSU, in the Texas Bowl. Finally, in 2022, Kansas State won the Big 12 Championship, validating our aggressively patient approach.

Ironically, just like it took me four long and patient years to reach the Northwestern Mutual 1% Forum, it also took Coach Klieman and the Wildcat football program four years to win a Big 12 Championship.

The lesson learned in both cases was that it could take a long time to succeed at anything meaningful. Many people give up way too early and never reach their full potential. That's disappointing because, as the Aggressive Patience Standard teaches us, steady and consistent improvement over an extended period tips the odds of winning whatever game you're playing heavily in your favor.

Most people understand the aggressive part. However, patience is often the more difficult part of the equation for this standard to work its magic. As long as you pound the stone long enough and hard enough, eventually, those stones will crumble beneath your unshakable will, and you'll have the victories you so richly deserve.

CHAPTER 7

The Expectations of Unexpected Intentional Touches

Most everyone who has ever been an employee goes through formal reviews to help document strengths and areas for improvement. If you're doing a good job, it either directly leads to a raise or a promotion. If you're not doing work that's up to snuff, you'll hear about that too, and you're generally given a plan to improve your efforts and results.

The same applies to all sports, such as baseball, where stats transparently measure your batting average, run production, defense, and dozens of other metrics. You'll know how well you're doing on the field by how much time you ride the bench or if you get sent down to the minors.

Let's face it; those reviews are brutal even when you're doing well because you're forced to hear just how well your performance is being perceived against a companywide, industrywide, or league-wide standard. Nobody likes formal performance reviews, either as a recipient or a manager, when delivering bad news is essential but often awkward.

Many people shy away from these reviews, and they're often delayed, especially with non-confrontational managers. That only worsens matters because, as an employee or a player, you're left wondering how you're doing in the eyes of those who control your immediate fate.

However, there is a better way. The Unexpected Intentional Touches Standard, UITS for short, is entirely the opposite of formal reviews you're subjected to every six months, annually, or when you slump for an extended time. I created the formal concept of the UITS several years ago when I saw the need to foster ongoing dialog when things were going poorly for my clients and when things were going well.

As the name implies, if you're in a leadership position, the UITS teaches you to find consistent and ongoing ways to provide feedback to those you lead. These can be small "atta boys" and "atta girls" that build confidence through praise when the recipient least expects it. For example, if you notice an employee staying late to put in extra work for one or more nights, signal out that extra effort. It's so easy to let small victories like that go in the constantly swirling, busy work environment. Still, it's that extra effort on your part that people take notice of with a ripple effect that will build loyalty and fire people up to seek more praise by looking for things big and small to propel the company's mission forward.

The UITS is a favorite of teachers who often deal with the fragile nature of small children. How many gold stars did you get on papers as a child? A shiny gold star invariably brightens your day because it feeds into your self-worth. Better yet, you could look forward to going home and receiving praise and maybe a coveted spot on the family refrigerator for your gold-star-worthy effort and results. The UITS in the adult world is no different.

Starting, you probably remember certain bosses you had who engaged in this activity. You gravitated to them because you wanted that recognition. You wanted the dopamine hit from feeling like your efforts are appreciated. Bosses who consistently praise your efforts are the ones you want to keep working for and who will inspire you to bring out your personal best.

The magic of the UITS is to implement it consistently but judiciously. Overindulging people with praise for every last thing diminishes the effect. Do not create a participation trophy culture! Using the UITS strategically, especially when you know someone needs a bump, which can turn an average employee into a superstar performer. Building better relationships using the UITS creates loyalty, fosters honesty, and encourages a higher degree of communication. It can also give much-needed guidance to let people under you know if they're on the right track instead of leaving them to guess if they're meeting or exceeding your expectations.

As a manager, you'll save time, money, and stress with unexpected intentional touches. All those things contribute to your organization's bottom line and ensure a healthier daily work life for all employees. If you're a CEO or senior leader, I strongly encourage you to build this into your organization's culture from top to bottom. It is a way to maintain healthy camaraderie in small doses that feed into and support your larger mission.

How the UITS Directly Impacted Me

Lynn Bozzay recruited me as a financial advisor at Northwestern Mutual in 2004. She worked out of St. Louis and had the reputation and results to back up her status as the top recruiter for Northwestern. It didn't take me long to see why.

That revelation didn't happen during the onboarding process. It happened after I was already a part of the firm. While she made me feel special during the hiring process, Lynn continued to stay in touch with me after I was already established as an advisor. That was despite her recruiting job and her complete contact with me.

John Qualy was my Managing Partner, and he created weekly printouts of how everyone on our team was doing, and Lynn always got a copy to keep tabs on the people she recruited into the company. She routinely sent me notes of encouragement and praise from these printouts, which greatly added to my feeling good about my efforts and results. She wasn't the only one who did this, but she stood out because she didn't have to stay in contact with me and several others, but she elevated her efforts to include the UITS Standard. Those small gestures compounded to help propel me to set national records for the fastest start at Northwestern Mutual.

The interesting thing about Lynn's notes was that they never focused on results. Her notes focused on the discipline and the discipline I had created to compete against more seasoned veterans who had been in the industry for years. She reinforced the things I was doing I could control instead of focusing on results that depended on the actions of others. Aside from the unexpected intentional touches, there was great wisdom in the types of things she also focused on.

All of this resulted in people wanting to know the secrets to my success. That's when I started being invited to speak at industry gatherings. Little did I know, but as good as I was at work in the financial services industry, I was even better and more passionate about becoming a peak performance coach. I will continue to write my best story because people like Lynn and John went over and above what they needed to do, contributing to the incredible life that I am now living.

I've seen the UITS also work wonders in locker rooms. I work with several college teams, and one of the critical culture-building exercises I encourage coaches to do is to reach out individually to players who are putting the extra effort by staying late to break down game film, spend extra hours in the weight room, or taking on leadership roles during practices. Most players, especially younger ones, are highly emotional, fueled by adrenaline to elevate their performances. Having a positive mindset and being surrounded by coaches and players who routinely contribute to that bottom line can mean everything for on-field and on-court performances.

Micro Touches at Microsoft

When I was the performance coach for the North Dakota State Bison football team, during one of the program's many championship runs, I met a man in the team hotel who was a big supporter of Bison football. He introduced himself as Leif Hemstad and said he flew into games from Austin, Texas. He noticed how I often frantically ran up and down the sidelines during games and knew I did mental conditioning for the Bison.

Leif was intrigued by my efforts, which helped lead to the team's success, and invited me to speak at his company. It turned out that the company was the Microsoft Solutions team, which did $7 billion in revenues. We started with a planning session at a retreat with twelve of his leaders who managed four hundred employees throughout North America.

In that planning session, we looked at areas of pain and opportunity. Based on feedback, we found all those leaders were struggling with communication issues because they had many other things on their agendas. In their minds, that lack of meaningful and ongoing communication undermined morale and diminished bottom-line results.

After hearing this, I quickly surmised that rather than adding a lot of heavy formal ways to connect, I taught them about the value of smaller micro connections in the form of unexpected intentional touches. I got them to buy into a simple and achievable goal. On average, each team leader managed forty people, and with twenty workdays in a month, all they needed to do was reach out to two employees daily. That extra ten minutes to give praise, recognition, and awareness had the potential to create an exponential return over the course of a year. And that's what happened.

When I met with Leif and his leaders at the end of the year, we conducted a detailed review of what worked best to drive improved performance, higher morale, and job satisfaction. Microsoft uses a standardized health score which is a compendium of all the company's metrics used to define the success and performance of individual business units. Leif and the Solutions business unit went from a challenging environment a year before to the highest health score in the world for all Microsoft divisions. There are a lot of elements that are used to create that health score. However, when we asked the team leaders what contributed most to the success of the entire unit, ten of the twelve leaders said it was implementing the UITS that brought their teams and the whole business unit to the next level.

The Unexpected Intentional Touches Standard works because it is simple and only requires that you are intentional and consistent in its application. That makes it one of the most effective ROI actions you can take.

CHAPTER 8

The Physical STANDARD

Doing Some Heavy Lifting with the Physical Standard

You can be as mentally tough as a honey badger, but if your body is as soft and squishy as bread dough, you'll never get everything you want in life. That's why one of the most important standards you can create for yourself is the Physical Standard.

Like all other standards, the Physical Standard requires a combination of education, dedication, and unwavering desire. It is especially transparent compared to the mental standards you set for yourself. That's because physical standards are the easiest for others to see and for you to measure your progress. Besides compliments from others, you can step on a bathroom scale every morning, take note when you tighten up your belt notch, and if you're going to the gym, you can measure times, weights, reps, and more to mark your progress.

Another important thing to remember about any physical standard is that with more energy, you'll have added focus, confidence, and a greater overall positive mental state. When you eat well and exercise correctly, your body triggers chemical reactions to optimize many other parts of your physical and mental well-being.

The physical standard is also a manifestation of how you attack every day. When operating at a peak physical capacity, you are better positioned to react to opportunities that come into your life when you least expect them. In short, an increased physical capacity translates into an increased overall capacity.

There are thousands of programs you can follow to achieve results, but it boils down to what has always been the case. You must create higher quality and quantity exercise and diet. The more active you are, the better your results will be. When you feed your physical engine the right fuels, you give it the tools it needs to optimize your efforts.

One of the components of your Physical Standard is to challenge yourself to achieve optimal growth to the point of making yourself uncomfortable. Just like anything else, be smart and know when enough is enough. You'll set yourself up for setbacks and failures if you overdo it.

Planking my Way to a Higher Physical Standard

We've all had those moments where we say we will start working out. We dig in with a lot of initial enthusiasm for the first few days and then get distracted. We decide it's more complicated than we thought and find excuses to stop. If that is you, don't beat yourself up because you're in good company. When we stop, it isn't that our physical standard is too hard. It simply means we haven't connected the right motivation to create the mental toughness to keep going. That's the secret sauce that spells the difference between success and failure.

You must develop a plan that works best for you physically and mentally. Many people create an initial 30-day challenge, which is a good starting point. However, if you'd like to amp up your efforts, I highly recommend my good friend Andy Frisella's book and program called *75 Hard*. It will change your physical body while it also changes your mental game. It's one of the best examples of a holistic approach to the Physical Standard I've used successfully.

When you create a physical standard, you're recalibrating many things. Perhaps the best lesson I ever got in how to do that was meeting David Goggins at an Alabama football training camp. David has transformed himself from overweight and uninspired to possibly the fittest human on the planet. His methods are uncompromising and, to some, a little extreme. As I've mentioned repeatedly, there can't be any compromise in a standard, and you need that uncomfortable, extreme element to produce the best results.

At Alabama's training camp, we were featured speakers, and during our downtime, we got to spend time together at the team's practices. One of David's keys to success is never letting his guard down. The man I saw on stage was the same man I talked to on the sidelines while the team was running drills. He and Coach Nick Saban are two of the most mentally locked-in people I've ever met. Working with them simultaneously created an unforgettable and intense experience for me.

I returned from that camp and started reading David's book, *Can't Hurt Me.* As part of his fitness strategy, David challenges readers to do one thing for thirty days to push themselves to new limits physically. I accepted that challenge, and the first thing that came to mind was planking.

For those who don't know, planking involves making your body as stiff as a board (or a plank) and staying in a challenging position for a predetermined amount of time, often off the floor with just a few body parts touching something to keep you in place. As somebody who has tried it, I guarantee it is harder than it sounds. If you search the Internet, you'll find thousands of highly entertaining examples.

As part of David's challenge, your goal is to increase your capacity gradually. In my case, I raised my planking time over the thirty days, starting with one minute, then two minutes, and quickly reaching four minutes, with my goal of planking for five minutes to complete the 30-day challenge.

I handled the first couple of days with no problem. Then I traveled to Sacramento for a speaking engagement with a financial firm. At dinner the night before, one of the senior executives asked me if he and a few others could work out with me in the morning. I welcomed the company, and since I was already working out hard, I used others joining me as added motivation. I needed to go even harder. They showed up, and we blew through our workout together.

Then I turned to them and said, "Now it's time to do the unrequired part of the workout. Let me introduce you to planking. I want each of you to plank for as long as you can. Push yourselves and see what happens."

I explained my goal of reaching five minutes by the end of the 30-day challenge by adding a few seconds each day after I reached a four-minute plateau. In turn, they challenged me by adding a few more seconds a day wasn't a real goal, and pushed me to try adding fifteen or thirty seconds a day. They put my own words back on me, saying, "Push yourself and see what happens."

So, for the next twenty-five days, that's precisely what I did. By pushing myself and finding my outer limits, at the end of the 30-day challenge, I planked for sixteen minutes.

I'm proud of that accomplishment, but the lesson here is that you never really know what you're capable of physically until you push yourself to your outer limits. The cool thing is that what you think your outer limits are and what they are can be quite different.

I also proved another of David's critical strategies in planking for sixteen minutes. In the SEAL community, you are taught the 40% rule. When you reach what you think is your breaking point, where you're exhausted and can't do more, you're taught that you've only used 40% of your capacity. You have 60% left in your tank that you didn't know existed.

When I set a goal of five minutes at the start of my planking challenge, little did I know that five minutes vs. the sixteen I achieved were less than 40% of what I could perform. With the right mental toughness mindset, I blasted through that five-minute mark and more than tripled what I thought I could do.

You have that same championship mindset in you, whether you realize it. Physical challenges and exercise are only one part of the Physical Standard. You need to feed your body the proper fuel if you also want to achieve the best results.

The Wedding Vow

Nutrition is often overlooked as a key to peak physical accomplishments, but it's as important as the right amount and kind of exercise. The motivation is the same. You must find something that matters enough so that you'll develop the mental discipline to succeed.

Here's a perfect example.

A few years ago, my friend Kaleb Thornhill, one of the vice presidents of the Miami Dolphins, started an organization called Pro-Athlete Community. His organization helps retired former Dolphins players re-acclimate to society after their playing days and he asked me to join him in working with some ex-players.

One participant was former Dolphins offensive lineman Ogemdi Nwagbuo who had ballooned up to 360 pounds from his playing weight of 315 pounds. During one of our intake sessions, he mentioned he would attend a wedding in three months and wanted to attend at his playing weight. That was a challenge but certainly achievable if he found the right motivation and put the right actions into motion. The wedding was important to Ogemdi and gave him the fuel to push hard against that deadline.

He knew he didn't need a fad diet or make crazy changes to hit that goal. As mentioned in another chapter, he needed something sustainable over a longer term and combined that with aggressive patience. In this case, the wedding was that sustainable goal.

When I asked Ogmedi about his eating habits, I was stunned by what he told me. He ate a full extra dinner every night besides his regular dinner. Seven extra dinners a week! That blew me away. However, that also made it easy to identify a change he could make to help him meet his goal.

I got Ogemdi to agree to eliminate one weekly dinner for the next seven weeks. He would eat only six extra dinners the first week. The second week, he would eat only five extra dinners, and so forth. I knew we had to build a long-term sustainable change to create a new habit to produce a new Physical Standard in his life. From there, we looked at who added to his eating woes by enabling lousy choices. Then we analyzed those bad food choices and replaced them with better options.

Those are difficult things to do when you love to eat, like most offensive linemen love to do.

However, that wedding was extremely important to Ogemdi, and when the ninety days were over, he sent me a picture of him at the wedding, wearing a suit from his playing days and weighing in at 315 pounds.

The longer-term payoff is that Ogemdi Nwagbuo continued his weight loss journey with these new habits in place and feels better than ever.

It's critical to remember that your Physical Standard is yours alone. Do not compare yourself to anyone else. Everyone has unique circumstances and genetics that contribute to their outcomes. Their physical standards are different from yours. Find your desired outcomes like David Goggins or that Dolphins player, and create the biggest and most meaningful reasons to drive your success.

Break a sweat every day. Be mindful of what you feed your body. Work with a trainer like many people do with my Uncommon Coaching live program. Get accountability partners or see if your insurance covers a nutritionist to help you create a sustainable plan.

Above all else, don't wait to implement a Physical Standard someday. Doing that means you'll only live with regrets later on.

CHAPTER 9

Strength Over Adversity

"Blessed is the one who perseveres under trial, for when they have stood the test will receive the crown of life that God has promised to those who love them."

James 1:12 NIV

Pain is a difficult but necessary teacher. Our greatest life lessons are not born from our successes. They are born during times of loss and adversity. Through this adversity, we become stronger versions of ourselves. We learn about our shortcomings and vulnerabilities and fight through that adversity when we put the most important standards in place. That is when we put a standard in place that triumphs over feelings. A standard that triumphs over pain and adversity and reminds us we are imperfect and vulnerable creatures but are still capable of doing great things.

This is the most difficult of all standards to master because we are born emotional beings and spend the rest of our lives learning how to process and control our feelings. In most cases, we master those feelings in certain times and situations. Feelings are always present and without a standard to reign in our feelings, we're left to the mercy of trying to cope with events, situations, tragedies, and relationships that can drain us and create bitterness. That doesn't need to be the case, but it often is.

What Holds You Back

Without exception, there is something inside of you that holds you back. It could be big, or it could be small, and you may not even be aware that it exists. Trust me, we all have emotional blockades that require our effort and attention if we are to minimize them. The key is developing the right mindset to drive accountability. We do this by learning how to control our emotions to create a mental environment that maximizes our strengths and minimizes the adversity we face. Much of this involves figuring out what we can control versus what we cannot.

When I work with high achievers, and we get on the topic of how to go to the next level, the question I always ask them is, "What holds you back?" I want to know what they think are their barriers to success. Sometimes, the answer is obvious. Sometimes, the people I ask are oblivious. They haven't thought much about it, and they can't come up with an answer that is on point and meaningful.

Although the thrust of my work is to help others attain their highest levels of performance, I also deal with the notion of what holds me back. Recently, I've thought more about this question, which concerns my relationship with my father.

My father, Burton Newman, passed away on November 5, 2022, and for the longest time, our relationship was distant and strained, framed because he and my mother divorced when I was six months old. The lack of a close and loving relationship with my father plagued me for many years, and privately, I battled with it daily.

One event from a few years ago reminded me of how poor that relationship was. In 2016, I gave a speech in Orlando to advisors in a financial services firm. One of the senior managers wanted to share insights with me, and as part of that conversation, he brought a new Tony Robbins documentary to my attention. At his urging, while at the airport waiting for my flight, I sat down in a bar, ordered a salad and a glass of water, cued up Netflix, and started watching. About twenty minutes in, Tony was dispensing advice at one of his mega events, and he asked a young woman to stand up and tell the audience what she thought was holding her back. I'll never forget her answer. She said something to the effect of "My dad did this, and my dad did that… and that's what's been holding me back in life."

Tony paused momentarily and then asked the woman if her father ever did anything positive for her in her life. "Of course," was the response, and the young woman reeled off several things that her father did that contributed positively to her life.

Tony's following words were like me touching a third rail on subway tracks. He said, "What if I shared that everything you've been through has made you who you are today? Do you understand these things your father did, good and bad, are giving you strength? You need to achieve whatever you want to achieve? All you have to do is shift your perspective."

I started bawling like a baby to where the bartender looked over and gave me an "Are you alright look," knowing I wasn't drinking but still having a tough moment.

Although Tony was talking to a young woman, he also talked to me. I sat there as a 37-year-old man, holding on to all my pain from a lifelong strained relationship with my dad. That day in the lounge and Tony's advice to that woman gave me the strength to overcome my adverse relationship with my dad. I thought about it for a couple of weeks and then called him.

I should preface things by making it known my dad was an angry and unstable man. It was challenging for me to be around him because he was short-tempered and abusive all the time, although he never physically laid a hand on me. His life was characterized by substance abuse and significant mental health issues. I won't sugarcoat things by saying his hurtful ways, and comments rolled off of me because they didn't. There was a lifetime of pain associated with my relationship with him, which made the phone call that day a tough thing to do. I did it anyway.

I had made a certain degree of peace with whom he was before that day. I dedicated myself to my work, family, and faith and found purpose in serving and helping others. Deep inside, my relationship with my father was an ugly scar that I carried with me for all of my life.

I said many things that day, but the one thing I remember most is these words. "Dad, there have been long periods in our relationship where I've been too hard on you, and for that, I'm sorry. You and I have been through a lot of tough stuff, some positive and some negative, but now I recognize those things have made me the man I am today, and I just wanted to thank you for that. I love you, Dad."

In a perfect world, my dad would have echoed similar sentiments. He would have forgiven me for any perceived transgressions and apologized for his shortcomings. He would have told me he loved me, too.

Instead, after a long pause, he said, "I think I'm gonna have to sit in my chair for a while. I never thought I'd receive a phone call like this." He hung up the phone.

Although it wasn't what I had hoped to hear, I hung up the phone that day and felt like the world had been lifted off my shoulders. I had chosen to control what I could control. I chose strength by telling my dad the truth, overcoming a lifetime of adversity that had characterized our relationship. My relationship with my father remained imperfect, but with that one action, I could figure out what was holding me back and take action to minimize how it was affecting my life. Even though my past actions weren't stellar, my conscience was clear because I had reframed my perspective.

Over the next few years, my father's health declined. At one point, several months before he passed, and we thought we would lose him in a matter of days, I went to the hospital because I wanted to make sure I said all the things I needed to say before he left this world. That day, I told him all I wanted was for him to be proud of me. He said nothing. I walked out of the hospital room that day, called my wife in tears, and asked her, "What the hell is wrong with him?"

Several months later, the day before he passed, I visited him in the hospital. As I was feeding him, we talked about a lot of things. Then he paused, and out of nowhere, he said, "I'm very proud of you."

I finally heard the words I had wanted to hear for my entire forty-three years of living. The ironic thing is that after I heard those words, I realized that all my life, I was seeking my father's validation, and as it turns out, I didn't need it. I understood at that moment that I was seeking a truth that wasn't true. I was worried about what someone else thought about me more than I thought of myself.

That lesson was a long time in coming. I couldn't control my dad's way of living. I could only control my thoughts and actions. Although I had known this for years, it didn't fully dawn on me until I lived it. That shift in perspective applies to all of us. Your mindset gives you the strength to overcome adversity. The Standard of Strength Over Adversity will serve you well once you master it.

The Way of the Wounded Warriors

A few years ago, I wrote a book called *Own Your Success*. It captured the attention of my high school friend, Ben Moses, who had become a surgeon at Fort Sam Houston in San Antonio, Texas. Ben loved the book so much that he asked me to bring copies as part of a speech he wanted me to make to 800 Wounded Warriors. Of course, I accepted immediately. I felt a strong sense of duty to give something back to the men and women of our armed forces who had already given so much to our country.

I have always been fascinated by the mental toughness it takes to put yourself where you're willing to make the ultimate sacrifice for a cause you believe in. I wanted to know more deeply how a soldier's burning purpose develops to the point that it compels them to risk everything, including death, without hesitation. I was going there to inspire these men and women, but inside, I can't tell you how much they had already inspired me.

This talk was different because while the stakes are high on playing fields and in boardrooms for the vast majority of the people I work with, facing potential adversity by putting your life on the line raised the stakes for this audience higher than any other I had ever spoken to at that point. Looking back, that remains the case to this day.

On the day of my speech, I walked into the hall. I faced an audience where every one of them had been torn apart physically, mentally, and emotionally by the horrors of their combat experience. I was uneasy and, in some ways, felt inadequate compared to the sacrifices each one had made on my behalf and for all Americans. Usually, I can read an audience, but I was taken aback on this day and wasn't quite sure what I'd see and hear.

First and foremost, I used the opportunity to thank those brave men and women for their sacrifice to protect the freedom of all

Americans. Even though they had paid a price, I reminded them that they were examples of courage and toughness that so many others could draw from. Surviving war, despite their wounds, was an ongoing testament to their perseverance and a consummate example of how using their strength to overcome adversity in this part of their lives would carry over as they transitioned to the next chapters in the coming years.

To cap things off, after my speech, I had the opportunity to watch one of the Wounded Warriors, Spc. Clayton Stockton received a Purple Heart. You have no idea what that feels like until you see it in person. Sgt. Maj. of the Army Jack Tilley oversaw the ceremony. As part of his presentation, he spoke about the commitment this warrior had displayed to his country, his dedication to his brother and sister soldiers, and his unwavering sense of duty to stay in the fight right up until the moment he stepped on an IED that blew off both of his legs from his body.

Despite his horrific injuries and adversity as he rebuilt his life and mangled body, that Warrior beamed with pride born from a love for his country. As he came to the podium, walking on two prosthetic legs, he stood tall and erect, knowing his cause was just and his purpose was meaningful.

I watched silently as the general placed the Purple Heart around his neck and invited Spc. Stockton to say a few words to his fellow Warriors. His voice never wavered as he said something that would stay with me for the rest of my life.

"If I had to go back and do it all over again the same way, without hesitation, that's what I would do. If the President allowed me to return to Afghanistan and fight right now, even missing two legs, that's exactly what I would do."

This was not a pep talk before a big game. It was not a sales director firing up a room full of advisors to keep working hard to make more sales. It was as real as it gets, with the highest stakes imaginable. You witness something like I did in that moment, which changes you. It changes you forever.

Despite his injuries, Spc. Stockton was the epitome of strength in overcoming adversity. I have thought back to that day often, and despite my challenges or when I help others with theirs, I refuse to feel sorry, knowing that others like him have overcome much more than I will probably ever face.

Spc. Stockton and that room full of Wounded Warrior's lesson for all of us is this. If you have doubts about your ability to overcome adversity, know that you are capable of incredible feats of mental and physical strength when your burn and your purpose are pure and potent. The Standard of Strength Over Adversity can be your most powerful asset. Study it and find a way to intentionally make it a part of your life when you need it most.

Like all other standards, and The Standard itself, how you choose to use them is strictly up to you. You decide how you show up in life. You decide what is important. You find clarity in your purpose and then, like Spc. Clayton Stockton, refuse to let any adversity get in your way.

Set your standards and live by them every moment of every day.

That's how you win in life.

CHAPTER 10

The Own It Mentality

By this point, you should thoroughly understand what The Standard is and how you can apply it to live your best life. I've cited several examples of using this philosophy and individual elements to create standards for all parts of your life. Now, only one thing remains.

You must choose to commit to a standards-based life. Nobody can do that for you. That's your moment of truth, and it's on you and nobody else. If you're going to set this book down or put it on a shelf somewhere, you haven't figured out the most important part of The Standard, so let me spell it out for you.

You must develop an *Own it Mentality.*

Talk is cheap. So is thinking if you don't act on what you want to get out of life. You must take charge and proactively decide that your life now isn't good enough for you. Once and for all, you must want change in your life bad enough that you're willing to commit to The Standard as a way of life. Everything else is something less.

For almost two decades, I've used many of the same tactics and strategies you've read about on these pages to help world champions, Hall of Famers, Fortune 500 CEOs, and wealthy individuals go to the next level to achieve legendary status. I've told you how many people have implemented The Standard to make that happen.

Your most important takeaway is that if you implement the things I've taught you here, you can also live your version of a legendary life. The Standard is universal. It applies to every person in every situation. That means it applies to you without reservation.

There are two final thoughts I want to leave you with that will help you begin your standards-based life and Own It Mentality. They're the final pieces to the puzzle and will give you the momentum to fortify your efforts and mindset.

Do What You Say You Will Do

For your talk to have value, you *must* do what you say you will do. The only way to do that with maximum effort and minimum headwinds is by connecting to your Burn. I have instructed people about the Burn since my earliest days as a peak performance coach.

Connecting to the Burn means finding the purpose and the reason that is so important to you that it smashes all resistance to barriers in your way. Consider Tom Brady's burn of winning Super Bowls or John Qualy connecting me to my mother's legacy to tap into my desire to be a top financial advisor at Northwestern Mutual.

Consider the burn that Ogemdi Nwagbuo attached to losing weight so that he could attend a wedding after dropping close to fifty pounds in three months. The Stonecutters Credo is another classic example of how, throughout history, people have attached outsized meanings to the difficult challenges they want to conquer.

A huge byproduct of doing what you say you will do is discipline, one of the most critical facets of any standard you create. You must be disciplined in keeping promises to yourself to have any chance of leading the life you deserve.

Only you know for sure what the burn is that lives inside you. It may be connected to being the best possible spouse, parent, or pillar in your community. Many link it to their faith, work, or passion for other quality-of-life pursuits. Again, the choice is yours. However, you must decide what that burn is and go after it with everything you've got.

When you do what you say you will do, you shift from an outcomes-based life that you don't control to a process-based life that you do control. In addition to everything else, that gives you more peace of mind and better health and makes you a better person in every relationship you have now and in the future.

When you do what you say you will do, it also means you can look in the mirror daily and know that you gave it your very best. Nobody can ever take that away from you.

Intentional Focus

Every person has some degree of focus they can summon to survive and thrive in this world. However, with a standards-based life, focus isn't enough. You must learn how to focus your focus, or as I call it, create Intentional Focus.

What's the difference?

The short answer is everything. Think of your ability to focus as a minimum requirement for entry into anything you do. For example, you must focus on hitting a baseball or meeting a monthly sales quota. If you want to hit stinging line drives and home runs or be the top producer in your company, you must go to the next level and break down your ability to focus even further.

Stanford professor Dr. Andrew Huberman explained it on one of his podcasts this way. Focus is your ability to see and acknowledge that you have shoes on your feet. Intentional focus is when you note how the shoes feel, fit, and look on you. When you walk, you note the comfort, support, and bounce the shoes provide. You lock in these observations that you may use later to help you decide whether or not to buy the same shoes, creating happier feet and more positive value in your life.

Here's a little secret for you. You've been wearing "shoes" in all parts of your life since the day you were born. In most cases, you're aware that you've got these shoes on, but most times, all you've done is check the box of shoes. When you apply intentional focus to the shoes in your life, you move forward with more discipline and awareness. You have lived this way for a long time, but until you're made aware of those shoes, you learn to settle and live with them, no matter how well they fit.

…

The Standard is time-tested and works, but only if you do the work as well. I can cite dozens of additional examples of how standards have produced wins for everyone who applies the required effort and execution.

What I can't do is decide to implement The Standard for you. That's your job. It's a gut check that is highly personal and unique only to you. I can work my butt off to help you, but I can't be you.

When YOU develop an *Own it Mentality* and choose to implement The STANDARD in YOUR life, you will write one helluva story and leave YOUR legacy.

Let's keep ATTACKING.

NOW. WE. GO.

Tools to ATTACK The STANDARD...

THE BURN

No matter what industry or discipline brought you here, YOUR next level must begin by addressing your belief in yourself.

In our work with some of the top athletes and business professionals in the world, we've uncovered that building unshakeable self-belief begins by connecting to what we call the **BURN**. The BURN drives these top performers to greatness. It goes deeper than just their WHY or their PURPOSE.

The Burn is what lights them up to believe anything is possible. It's the mindset that causes them to fight on a different level.

I'm a firm believer that the same Burn lies inside each and every single one of YOU.

Uncovering and connecting to it consistently will light YOUR why on fire and drive YOU to take the necessary actions.

The Burn in your heart, that underlying passion, will help YOU fight through anything in your life and emerge on a different plane than where YOU started.

My deep inner passion to constantly become the best version of myself stems from a few things. However, my biggest driving force (BURN) is to carry on the LEGACY that my mother left behind when she died of a rare muscle disease when I was only eight.

She lived in a way that was so selfless and incredibly profound that I've crafted my life around the lessons she left me inside of a blue mead notebook. I have created an environment to remind myself of that every day.

My Burn will always be the same - to continue writing my mother's story. It will never change and always cause me to show up differently.

This may not be the case for everyone. For some, their Burn may be materialistic, but it's important to recognize a materialistic Burn is temporary.

If it's going to be a goal or something you're fighting for, once you reach it, you must redefine and reconnect to something deeper.

That being said, it's also okay if your Burn changes over time based on your different stages of life, adversities you may face, etc.

This is not rocket science. There is no equation to finding the perfect Burn, and it's not something you are glued to from here on out.

All that matters is you understand your Burn and connect to it daily. You will create an environment that drives accountability and causes YOU to do what it takes.

This is about attacking the next level and becoming YOUR best self. **The Burn ignites it all.**

Use this area to brainstorm ideas of what YOU think YOUR Burn might be…

Want to hear how some of the highest performers in the world connect to their Burn?

Check out The Burn Podcast on all podcast platforms and YouTube!

www.bennewman.net/theburn/

Now that you've explored your Burn, I have a challenge for YOU.

Over the next **thirty days,** I want you to challenge yourself to connect to your unique Burn every single day using what I call, "The Burn Journal Challenge." Now, you can use a physical journal (how I do it) or start a journal on your phone. Whatever works for you. Every morning for the next thirty days, you will write your Burn in this journal and connect to it.

This will help you decide if the Burn you wrote down is powerful enough or if you need to dig a little deeper. When you've genuinely uncovered what your current Burn is, you will be flooded with energy and passion for taking the necessary action in your daily life.

Your greatest level of performance relies on your ability to connect to your true Burn.

STEP 1: YOUR ALARM

I'm not saying you have to wake up at the same time I do every day, but whenever you set YOUR alarm clock, go in and rename the alarm to YOUR Burn. Mine says, "Janet Fishman Newman. LEGACY." After seeing that, there's no way I'm hitting snooze. I lock in, and I'm ready to ATTACK.

STEP 2: THE JOURNAL

Grab a small journal or notebook and commit to writing down your Burn every morning for the next 30 days. This is what I mean by "connecting" to your Burn. This will help YOU build an environment that it takes to connect consistently to this inner FIRE and allow it to light up YOUR actions to a whole new level of consistency.

How are YOU showing up every day??

Choosing Passion for the Process over Results.

Daily routines are the backbone of building the type of life that YOU want. The problem is that far too many people focus on results-based activities when building a daily routine.

We will help YOU build the proven daily HABIT builder called "Your Prizefighter Day."

I have used this strategy for years and taught it to thousands of high performers.

We're going to break down the actual daily habits and disciplines that are going to help you ATTACK the most important things in YOUR life.

THE KEY: The Prizefighter Day is not just another daily routine. It's an ACTION plan. It's been proven that to reach your highest performance levels, you have to become obsessed with the process and not the results. The Prizefighter Day brings together the three areas of life that have been proven to have the most significant impact. Remember, these are not goals. These are ACTIONS. I've included some examples below to get you in the right mindset to build your own Prizefighter Day.

1. PERSONAL ACTIVITY EXAMPLE:

Waking up every morning and getting in your morning workout (because it releases endorphins and builds confidence).

2. BUSINESS OR ATHLETIC ACTIVITY EXAMPLE:

Setting a specific goal for the number of phone calls/ follow-ups/ reps/ workouts that you have to make every day, knowing that will further your success, regardless of the results.

3. SERVICE TO OTHERS EXAMPLE:

This could be lending an ear to a friend, complimenting a stranger, calling your parents, etc. What activity can you consistently do in the service of others?

Take your time. After watching the video, create your three focal points that are activity-driven to give you a sense of accomplishment in creating a balanced life, both personally and professionally.

Before you know it, you will gradually start to pull away from old disempowering conversations, noting that even an "ordinary" day is a ***Prizefighter Day*** on your path to greatness.

YOUR Prizefighter Day

Your BEST results come from periods when you're completely locked in on a process - NOT results. The sooner you uncover those daily disciplines that make the biggest difference in YOUR life, the faster your goals will manifest in front of YOUR face. Take your time and fill in each box with what YOU feel is the most important ACTION in each area of your life.

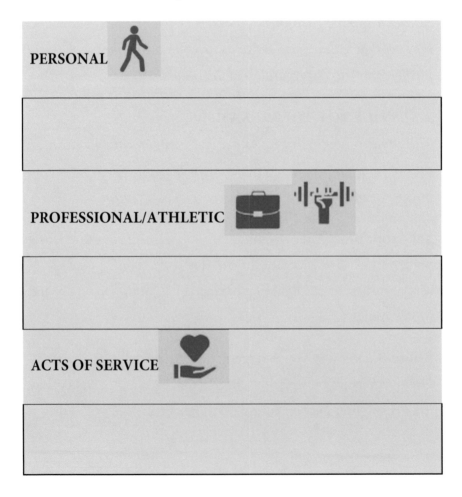

"I learned while at Alabama that you have Prizefighter Days. When stacking Prizefighter days, you develop the uncommon mindset. You prepare to attack the field, and you take an uncommon mindset to the game. You see, high levels of success are uncommon. Sustaining them is even more uncommon. Prizefighter Days prepare you to attack the big goals that you create, which allows you to reach peak performance."

- Mac Jones

2x National Champion with Alabama Football,

Davey O'Brien Award Winner & Heisman Finalist,

New England Patriots Quarterback

Stay connected to daily motivation to drive consistency on YOUR Prizefighter Day. #ATTACKthePROCESS

When I talk to people about succeeding in the significant personal and professional goals in their lives, I always start by focusing on three things.

Purpose, Process, and Reframing.

Are you staying connected to the purpose that will cause you to take significant action?

Are you staying connected to the process--not focusing on results you can't control--that will drive success in your life?

Are you reframing your goal by staying focused on solutions rather than problems?

Success means overcoming challenges, adversity, and hardship. Focusing on purpose, process, and reframing gives you the tools to overcome these challenges.

When I introduce these concepts to people, it invariably leads to two questions.

What makes the greatest great?

What makes the best performers the best?

Focus on a Standard vs. Feelings.

To truly be the best of the best, high achievers don't allow feelings to dictate how they show up.

We all go through tough times in our lives. But the greatest of the great accept those setbacks. They embrace challenges as part of life. And if the purpose is significant enough, they continue to fight with everything they have.

But many others show up and allow feelings to dictate their performance.

That's why the most successful people live to a standard and not to their feelings.

The Work Out Example.

Here's a perfect example of how a standard vs. feelings can impact your life. You can apply this simple illustration to everything you do.

Let's say you decide to start a new workout program. On Day One, the alarm goes off at 6 a.m. But because that warm bed and soft sheets feel so good, you snuggle in, hit the snooze button, and go back to sleep.

"Heck, it's only the first day," you tell yourself, "I can always start tomorrow."

You hit the snooze button a couple more times, and before you know it, there's not enough time to get up and start your new routine. That is a perfect example of living to your feelings.

But if you realize the benefits of getting up and out of bed and committing to a workout is going to make you healthier, feel better and have more energy, you will recognize this standard is important enough to wipe the sleep from your eyes, gladly hop out of bed, and dig right into your morning workout.

Belief. Potential. Action. Results.
Many people think that the most successful people have found a way to skip ahead, to go around the process that is required to be successful. They're wrong.

Success is simply the direct result of hard work.

To put people in the right frame of mind about what it takes to set a standard that incorporates hard work, I ask people to think about four elements -- belief, potential, actions, and results.

Having a **belief** in yourself is the first key to achieving success. Underperformers almost always don't believe in themselves enough or in their purpose in life. Assuming that you can succeed in whatever task is before you is the first challenge you must meet.

If you don't have a complete belief in yourself, it is impossible to access the full **potential** you have. When you create a barrier that walls off a belief that you can achieve your goal, by extension, you automatically also wall off the total amount of potential as well.

Without a strong enough belief that limits the ability to tap into our full potential, what will your **actions** look like? As you can guess, they will be less than what you are fully capable of executing.

This underperformance means our results will be less than we had hoped for.

And when our results are less than we had hoped for, our feelings come into play. We begin to doubt ourselves. We undermine our potential. This leads us back to substandard actions and poorer results yet again.

If you implement these core actions, you will enjoy greater success. But there is one landmine you need to be careful of as you go about your business. I call this the **seduction of success**.

Simply put, it means that after enjoying a certain measure of success, some people decide to ease up, take time off, and coast for a while, enjoying what success they have already achieved.

When you do this, you're fooling yourself into believing you're living up to your full potential. But you're not. True high achievers are never seduced by success.

Jerry Rice and the 100 Percent Choice.

If anyone knows about being a high achiever, it's wide receiver Jerry Rice. When Jerry and I shared a stage in Las Vegas a few years ago, exchanging ideas in the green room before we went on, he said, "You know what I've never understood? How could somebody not give 100 percent when it is 100 percent their choice?"

Simple but profound. If ever you wanted an example of what it means to live to a standard vs. living through your feelings, that is it.

Jerry was never seduced by success. Like other high achievers, he recognized what made him feel good was his belief in himself and how it allowed him to reach his full potential, optimal actions, and superior results.

Taking Responsibility.

If we aren't getting the results we want, it's not because of how the world has treated us; it is because of the choices we've made. We are responsible for our own decisions and our actions.

When we fall short, it's because *we* didn't believe enough in ourselves. *We* didn't tap into our full potential. *We* didn't take the actions to drive the results we wanted to get.

I define winning a bit differently than most people as a result. To me, winning is the direct result of the quality of your actions. You can't always control the final score or the outcome, so I define winning as giving it your best at all times. If you can say that you gave it everything you had, whatever you do, nobody can take that away from you.

The 4 P's of
THE STANDARD

#STANDARDoverFEELINGS   #ATTACKthePROCESS

That's winning. And you can never ask any more of yourself than that.

You must be responsible for continuous focus on purpose, process, and reframing, doing the same things over and over and over again with grit and perseverance. If you do, the story you write for your life will stagger your imagination.

More Books by Ben...

"UNCOMMON Leadership"

#1 Wall Street Journal & USA Today Best Seller!

In *Uncommon Leadership*, performance coach and motivational consultant Ben Newman takes you inside the minds and hearts of eleven exceptional individuals: athletes, coaches, CEOs, entrepreneurs, and others whose unrelentingly high performance has made them not only the best in their fields but also unquestioned leaders in sports, business, and life. Ben breaks it down, honing in on the core qualities that drive these trailblazers to push for the best in themselves and others, every single day.

If you're looking for more in your life-your career, your relationships, your industry, or your personal performance-Ben Newman's *Uncommon Leadership* will give you the keys you need to unlock your best self. You'll learn how to adapt the principles of proven leaders to maximize your own potential. You'll see how some of today's top-performing people have tapped into their own core strengths, and with Ben's advice, you'll gain focus for identifying and tapping into yours.

If you want to unleash the champion inside you, there's no better way than to study and imitate other champions who have paved the way. Let Ben Newman's *Uncommon Leadership* give you the inside track to becoming all that you can be.

"I learned while at Alabama that you have Prizefighter Days. When stacking PrizeFighter days, you develop the uncommon mindset. You prepare to attack the field and you take an uncommon mindset to the game. You see, high levels of success are uncommon. Sustaining them is even more uncommon. Prizefighter Days prepare you to attack the big goals that you create which allows you to reach peak performance."

Mac Jones
2x National Champion with Alabama Football, Davey O'Brien Award Winner & Heisman Finalist, New England Patriots Quarterback

"YOUR Mental Toughness Playbook"

One of the first rules of sports psychology for an athlete to perform at their highest level is that they can't solely rely on their natural talents and abilities. Instead, they have to understand the mental toughness side of what it takes to achieve peak performance. I believe this concept applies to ALL individuals fighting to achieve peak performance in their lives.

This playbook and video series is about embracing the fact that your success is not just about changing your habits. It's about changing the way that YOU think. The most successful people are those who exemplify the importance of combining great habits and passion for the process with their ability to embrace adversity and challenge; to remain strong in driving their goals to completion.

In this program we will explore six rounds of YOUR mental toughness including YOUR Burn and Attaining Belief in Yourself, The Power to REFRAME, YOUR "I AM" Statements, YOUR Prizefighter Day, YOUR Legacy Statement, and Creating YOUR Environment for Greatness. These tools have seen proven results and led to championships with athletes at all levels and across many sports as well as with Fortune 500 executives and top business professionals and companies all over the world.

This playbook will test your mental toughness and empower you to attack your fears, push your comfort zones, and drive you to achieve peak performance by identifying your passion for the process of what you do. Often times we hold on too tightly to results that we can't control rather than identifying the daily behaviors that will drive performance. YOU will learn to shift YOUR mindset to focus on the process that will drive YOUR success.

"The most successful athletes and business leaders in the world have mental toughness and an "it" factor that allows them to achieve at the highest level. Ben Newman's tools and techniques make him one of the best in the world at helping people gain that edge."

Drew Hanlen
Top NBA Skills Trainer

"Leave YOUR Legacy: The Power to Unleash YOUR Greatness"

Learn to live a truly exceptional life with the help of author, speaker, and performance coach Ben Newman. In *Leave YOUR Legacy*, you will see firsthand how to drive impact by changing your perspective and connecting to your life's purpose.

Newman shows you how to be your best self with this touching story that clearly illuminates the steps needed to create major change in your life by following the ups and downs of the protagonist, Pierce. Join Pierce on his journey to greatness--from the humble beginnings of enacting change and resisting old behaviors to the reframing of his thoughts and actions and eventually understanding his legacy.

"Own Your Success connects you to your life's purpose. Leave YOUR Legacy will redefine your thinking to embrace change and leave an impact on others."

Will Compton
NFL Linebacker
Former Washington Redskins Defensive Captain

"Own YOUR Success: The Power to Choose Greatness and Make Every Day Victorious"

~National Bestseller and named by CEO Read as their #13 Business Book of 2012!

What if you could make each and every day victorious by focusing on daily activities rather than obsessing over results that you can't control? Based on author Ben Newman's popular program, *Own YOUR Success* gives you the power to make each day a triumph. The most successful people find great success when they focus on having a passion for the process. The key: make today victorious regardless of the obstacles that come your way. Figure out what fires YOU up without exception and ignite that passion so that you can routinely create your prizefighter day.

Own YOUR Success will lead you to uncover your true potential and create a life that belongs to YOU.

"I firmly believe that we are where we are in life because of our choices. Being great is also a choice and it helps if there are resources that would help us understand the process that causes one to be great. Well now you have it! Own Your Success is one of those resources. Read it and it will help you release your potential."

Aeneas Williams
NFL Hall-of-Fame Cornerback
14 year NFL Veteran and 8 time Pro-bowler

"Fight the Good Fight: A Mother's Legacy Lives On"

Fight the Good Fight provides inspiration for individuals who choose to embrace adversity in order to reach success. Over twenty years ago Ben Newman suffered the loss of his mother after years of watching her health deteriorate. After her tragic passing, his grandmother gave him an unexpected gift, in the form of a journal his mother left behind... A journey that is poignant, emotional, and sometimes heartbreaking, this is a story that you will remember forever in your soul.

"Fight the Good Fight is one of those quick reads that I had trouble putting down. The heart gets involved as Ben Newman exposes his own, with the tragedies that motivated him to help others. The idea of persistence, and legacy are right on track with every successful athlete and business man I know, and the insights in this book will hit the competitor in each of us, right between the eyes."

Mike Matheny
Former Manager of the St. Louis Cardinals and Kansas City Royals

"Pocket Truths for Success: 365 Daily Principles to Become the Most Successful Person You Know"

Pocket Truths for Success is your succinct guide to establishing priorities and achieving success in life. *Pocket Truths for Success* was written to be an inspiration for anyone facing the seemingly insurmountable challenges on the road to life's great successes. Personally and professionally, success is a difficult endeavor and possibly even harder to sustain once achieved. This book was written to address the two pivotal issues of achieving and sustaining success, in the complex ever-changing world we live in today. *Pocket Truths* delivers simple and powerful quotes for those ready to inspire and lead.

"Pocket Truths will inspire you to lead yourself, to lead others, and to make positive waves of change in the future. This book will concisely enable you to define your LEGACY!"

Jon Gordon
New York Times Bestseller of "The Energy Bus"

Be Empowered to ATTACK The STANDARD...

The Ben Newman Companies, a professional speaking and consulting company, works with organizations and teams all over the world.

Our customized speaking and coaching leave audiences inspired, educated, AND empowered! Participants can uncover their true potential, readying them to create the life they are meant to fight for and enjoy and emerging poised to take on THEIR relentless pursuit of GREATNESS.

THE BEN NEWMAN COMPANIES

WHAT WE OFFER:

1-ON-1 PERFORMANCE COACHING

GROUP & LEADERSHIP PERFORMANCE COACHING

COACHING SYSTEMS • KEYNOTES • SEMINARS • TRAININGS

MEDIA SOLUTIONS & PACKAGES

LIVE EVENTS & BOOT CAMPS

If YOU are interested in partnering with us, please contact
The Ben Newman Companies at info@BenNewman.net.

STAY CONNECTED WITH BEN & OUR TEAM:

 @ContinuedFight   Ben Newman

 Ben Newman | The Burn    info@BenNewman.net    www.BenNewmanCoaching.com
www.BenNewman.net

About the Author...

Meet Ben Newman. You may have seen him running up the sidelines as a Mental Performance Coach for your favorite sports team or recognize him for his bestselling book UNCOMMON Leadership.

He's an Entrepreneur, Investor, #1 *Wall Street Journal* and *USA Today* Bestselling Author, Philanthropist, **AND THE NATION'S TOP CONTINUAL PEAK PERFORMANCE COACH.**

Internationally-Renowned Speaker. Ben's authentic, powerful, and engaging storytelling has become internationally recognized, and has been a featured speaker at the world's biggest business, sports, finance, and motivational events. He has shared the stage with Jerry Rice, Ray Lewis, Colin Powell, Ed Mylett, Jackie Joyner-Kersee, Jon Gordon, Tim Grover, Eric Thomas, Tony Dungy, Brian Tracy, Jenna Kutcher, and other legends worldwide. **Ben was selected by Influencive.com as one of the TOP 10 Motivators in Sports, and Real Leaders Magazine selected him as one of their TOP 50 Speakers in the World for the last four years.**

Performance and Mental Conditioning Coach for some of today's greatest professional athletes and highest-performing teams in the NFL, NBA, PGA, MLB, UFC, and NCAA. Ben has worked with coaches and players from the last six Super Bowl Champion teams.

He serves as the Performance Coach for the Big 12 Champion Kansas State football team in his 9th season (3 National Championships at North Dakota State) with Head Coach Chris Klieman. Ben also serves as the Performance Coach for Michigan State University's football and basketball program with Coach Mel Tucker and Coach Tom Izzo. Lastly, he served five years as the Mental Conditioning Coach for the 18-time National Champion football team Alabama Crimson Tide.

For the last two decades, Ben has served as the Peak Performance Coach for the top 1% of financial advisors globally and Fortune 500 business executives. Ben's clients have included: Microsoft, United States Army, Anheuser-Busch InBev, Quicken Loans, MARS Snackfoods, AstraZeneca, Northwestern Mutual, AFA Singapore, Mass Financial Group, Frontier Companies, Wells Fargo Advisors, Great West Life Canada, Boston Medical Center, Boys & Girls Club of America, New York Life as well as thousands of executives, entrepreneurs, athletes, and sales teams from around the globe.

Millions of people and some of the top performers in the world have been empowered by Ben through his books, educational content, coaching programs, podcast, and live events.

Ben is also the host of the top podcast, The Burn, where he takes you into the minds of some of the highest performers in sports and business to tell their whole story.

Ben lives in his hometown of St. Louis, Missouri, with the true measure of his success, his wife, Ami, and their children, J. Isaac and Kennedy Rose.

"YOUR success is not just about changing YOUR habits; it's about changing the way YOU think."

-Ben Newman

Ben Newman
The Ben Newman Companies
www.BenNewman.net

Acknowledgments...

The Standard is my eighth book, and I've thanked many others in previous publications. My gratitude remains as deep as ever for those who have helped me through their love, support, thoughts, words, and encouragement. YOU know who YOU are.

My greatest SUCCESS will always be my fight to live to the STANDARD as a father and husband. J. Isaac and Kennedy Rose, I would do anything and sacrifice anything for YOU. YOU will always get my best. EVERY. DAY.

However, none of my success and happiness in life would be possible without the love and support of my wife, Ami. I dedicate this book, and so much more, to her.

Ami has lived to all the principles in The Standard, from growing up in the small town of Edinburgh, Illinois, to creating a powerful and dynamic 23-year career as a leader at Anheuser-Busch InBev before retiring in 2021. She is a fighter who sets an example for our family and pushes all of us. She is the glue.

In 18+ years of traveling the world to coach and speak, standing on a sideline every weekend during football season, or coaching people with a relentlessly demanding schedule, Ami has never said NO. Not once. Ever. She has always had my back and done what needed to be done for our children, our home, and our family. She is the STANDARD of love, commitment, and doing what it takes.

My career success would not have been possible without her support, strength, and resilience.

Thank you, Ami. I love you with all my heart, and I'm so excited to spend the rest of my life with YOU.

To purchase bulk copies of any of Ben's books at a discount for large groups or your organization, please contact info@BenNewman.net